Windows Programming
with C++

Addison-Wesley Nitty Gritty

PROGRAMMING SERIES

Windows Programming with C++

Henning Hansen

ADDISON-WESLEY

An imprint of Pearson Education

Boston • San Francisco • New York • Toronto • Montreal • London • Munich
Paris • Madrid • Cape Town • Sydney • Tokyo • Singapore • Mexico City

PEARSON EDUCATION LIMITED

Head Office
Edinburgh Gate, Harlow, Essex CM20 2JE
Tel: +44 (0)1279 623623 Fax: +44 (0)1279 431059

London Office
128 Long Acre, London WC2E 9AN
Tel: +44 (0)20 7447 2000 Fax: +44 (0)20 7240 5771
Websites:
www.it-minds.com   www.aw.com/cseng

First published in Great Britain 2002
© Pearson Education Limited 2002

First published in 2001 as *Windows-Programmierung mit C++ Nitty-Gritty*
by Addison-Wesley Verlag, Germany.

The rights of Henning Hansen to be identified as Author of this Work have been
asserted by him in accordance with the Copyright, Designs and Patents Act 1988.

Library of Congress Cataloguing Publication Data
Applied for.

British Library Cataloguing in Publication Data
A CIP catalogue record for this book can be obtained from the British Library.

ISBN 0-201-75881-4

The programs in this book have been included for their instructional value. The
publisher does not offer any warranties or representations in respect of their fit-
ness for a particular purpose, nor does the publisher accept any liability for any
loss or damage arising from their use.

10 9 8 7 6 5 4 3 2 1

Translated and typeset by Berlitz GlobalNET (UK) Ltd. of Luton, Bedfordshire.
Printed and bound in Great Britain by Biddles Ltd. of Guildford and King's Lynn.

The publishers' policy is to use paper manufactured from sustainable forests.

Contents

Part I – Start up!   I

1   Introduction   3
  1.1   General information   3
    1.1.1   Requirements   3
    1.1.2   The objective of the manual   3
    1.1.3   Using compilers   3
  1.2   The first application   5
    1.2.1   Off we go!   5
    1.2.2   Explanation of the source code   7
  1.3   General information on objects   16
  1.4   Note   16

2   Introduction to the GDI   17
  2.1   What is the GDI?   17
  2.2   The GDI program   18
    2.2.1   The source code   18
    2.2.2   Explanation of the source code 21

3   Displaying text using the GDI   31
  3.1   General information   31
  3.2   Creating text using the GDI   32
    3.2.1   The source code   32
    3.2.2   Explanation of the source code 35

4   Control elements   41
  4.1   General information   41
  4.2   An application   41
    4.2.1   The source code   41
    4.2.2   Explanation of the source code 46

5   The edit field control element   53
  5.1   General information   53
  5.2   An application   53
    5.2.1   The source code   53
    5.2.2   Explanation of the source code 61

6	**System shutdown**		**65**
6.1	General information		65
6.2	An application		65
	6.2.1	The source code	65
	6.2.2	Explanation of the source code	73
7	**Bitmaps**		**75**
7.1	General information		75
	7.1.1	DDB	75
	7.1.2	DIB	75
	7.1.3	Color depth	76
7.2	The DDB application		76
	7.2.1	The source code	76
	7.2.2	Explanation of the source code	81
7.3	The DIB application		85
	7.3.1	The source code	85
	7.3.2	Explanation of the source code	88
8	**Menus**		**93**
8.1	General information		93
8.2	An application		94
	8.2.1	The source code	94
	8.2.2	Explanation of the source code	101
9	**Handling files**		**109**
9.1	General information		109
	9.1.1	File systems	109
	9.1.2	Functions	109
9.2	An application		109
	9.2.1	The source code	109
	9.2.2	Explanation of the source code	115
10	**Applications, processes and threads**		**119**
10.1	General information		119
10.2	A multi-threading application		119
	10.2.1	The source code	119
	10.2.2	Explanation of the source code	123
11	**DLL files**		**125**
11.1	General information		125
11.2	An application		126
	11.2.1	The source code	126
	11.2.2	Explanation of the source code	129
12	**Timers**		**131**
12.1	General information		131

12.2	An application with timer messages	131
12.2.1	The source code	131
12.2.2	Explanation of the source code	134
12.3	An application with a timer function	135
12.3.1	The source code	135
12.3.2	Explanation of the source code	137

13 The printer — **139**

13.1	General information	139
13.2	An application	139
13.2.1	The source code	139
13.2.2	Explanation of the source code	143

Part II – Take that!   147

14 Win32 API: Data types — **149**

| 14.1 | General information | 149 |
| 14.2 | Table | 149 |

15 Functions, structures, messages, and objects of the Win32 API — **151**

| 15.1 | General information | 151 |

16 Win32 API: Windows fundamentals — **153**

16.1	Win32 API functions, structures, messages, and objects for Windows fundamentals	153
16.1.1	Window object	154
16.1.2	CreateWindow	154
16.1.3	WM_CREATE	157
16.1.4	CREATESTRUCT	158
16.1.5	DestroyWindow	159
16.1.6	WM_DESTROY	159
16.1.7	ShowWindow	160
16.1.8	GetMessage	161
16.1.9	PeekMessage	162
16.1.10	RegisterClass	164
16.1.11	WNDCLASS	164
16.1.12	TranslateMessage	167
16.1.13	DispatchMessage	168
16.1.14	WM_PAINT	168
16.2	Examples	169
16.2.1	Creating a normal window	169

17 Win32 API: GDI   **173**

17.1   Win32 API functions, structures, messages, and objects for the GDI   173

         17.1.1   Device context object   176

         17.1.2   BeginPaint   176

         17.1.3   EndPaint   177

         17.1.4   PAINTSTRUCT   178

         17.1.5   GetDC   178

         17.1.6   ReleaseDC   179

         17.1.7   GetWindowDC   180

         17.1.8   SetPixel   180

         17.1.9   GetPixel   181

         17.1.10   MoveToEx   181

         17.1.11   POINT   182

         17.1.12   LineTo   183

         17.1.13   PolyLine   183

         17.1.14   PolyBezier   184

         17.1.15   Rectangle   185

         17.1.16   FillRect   185

         17.1.17   RECT   186

         17.1.18   Ellipse   186

         17.1.19   CreatePen   187

         17.1.20   Pen object   188

         17.1.21   SelectObject   188

         17.1.22   DeleteObject   189

         17.1.23   CreateSolidBrush   189

         17.1.24   Brush object   190

         17.1.25   TextOut   190

         17.1.26   SetTextColor   191

         17.1.27   SetBkColor   191

         17.1.28   SetTextAlign   192

         17.1.29   SetBkMode   193

         17.1.30   RGB   194

         17.1.31   CreateRectRgn   194

         17.1.32   Region object   195

         17.1.33   CombineRgn   195

         17.1.34   SetWindowRgn   196

         17.1.35   GetStockObject   197

         17.1.36   DrawText   198

17.2   Examples   200

         17.2.1   Finding a graphics area in the WM_PAINT message and drawing something in it   200

	17.2.2	Creating and assigning Pen and Brush objects	202
	17.2.3	Displaying text	205
	17.2.4	Using regions	208

18 Win32 API: File management — **211**

18.1	Win32 API functions, structures, messages, and objects for file management		211
	18.1.1	CreateFile	212
	18.1.2	CloseHandle	215
	18.1.3	ReadFile	215
	18.1.4	WriteFile	216
	18.1.5	CopyFile	217
	18.1.6	DeleteFile	218
	18.1.7	MoveFile	218
18.2	Examples		219
	18.2.1	Creating a simple file and filling it with data	219
	18.2.2	Opening a simple file and reading data from it	219

19 Predefined window classes — **221**

19.1	General information		221
	19.1.1	BUTTON	222
	19.1.2	EDIT	232
	19.1.3	List box	250
	19.1.4	Static	253

Part III – Go ahead! — **257**

20 DirectX — **259**

20.1	General information		259
20.2	A DirectX program		259
	20.2.1	General information	259
	20.2.2	The source code	260
	20.2.3	Explanation of the source code	264
20.3	DirectX and bitmaps		265
	20.3.1	General information	265
	20.3.2	The source code	266

21 UNICODE — **273**

21.1	General information		273
21.2	Operating systems		273
	21.2.1	Windows 95	273

	21.2.2	Windows 98	273
	21.2.3	Windows NT	273
	21.2.4	Windows 2000	274
	21.2.5	Windows CE	274

22 COM — **275**

22.1	General information	275
22.2	DirectX	275

23 Resources — **277**

23.1	General information	277
23.2	An example of a resource	277
	23.2.1 General information	277
	23.2.2 Explanation	280

Index — *281*

Part I

Start up!

Introduction

1.1 General information

1.1.1 Requirements

You need to have a good knowledge of the C++ language. You also need a C++ compiler with Windows libraries. All the examples given in this manual can be compiled using MS Visual C++ 6.0 and Borland Compiler C++ 5.5. The Borland compiler is available free of charge on the Internet and can be downloaded from the Borland homepage (www.inprise.com).

1.1.2 The objective of the manual

This manual is designed to enable you to write your own Windows programs. To do this, you need to have some internal knowledge of the Windows architecture because this is the only way to create professional programs. This manual is based on Windows 98. Since the other Windows versions are quite similar, however, the information given here can easily be applied to the other versions.

1.1.3 Using compilers

Borland C++ 5.5

Install this compiler on your hard disk in the C:\BCC55 directory on a different directory of your own choice. The compiler does not have a graphic interface, so you must therefore call the compiler in *DOS*. Use the *MS-DOS Prompt* in Windows to do this.

Go to the C:\BCC55 directory on drive C:. Create a new directory there called \IN and then create another directory called \OUT. You can create applications under *MS DOS* using the command md directory name. To create a directory in *Windows Explorer*, simply choose FOLDER in the FILE | NEW menu and enter a name.

➔ Return to the C:\BCC55 directory and change to C:\BCC55\IN. Create a batch file called compile.bat in this directory. Use the *MS-DOS editor* to create the batch file. Start the editor with Edit. At the end of this point, you see the contents of the batch file. You must copy the contents exactly as it appears here. Naturally, you must change the relevant directory names if you selected a different installation directory. Now, enter the following line in the batch file:

```
C:\BCC55\BIN\BCC32.EXE -tW -IC:\BCC55\INCLUDE
    -LC:\BCC55\LIB -nC:\BCC55\OUT %1 %2 %3
```

➔ All the parameters have an important meaning. The -tW parameter indicates that it is a Windows program. The -I... parameter specifies the directory for the include files (e.g. for WINDOWS.H). The -L... parameter indicates the directory for the lib files (e.g. for STDLIB.LIB). The %1 %2 ... parameters indicate that three parameters, which are transferred to this batch file, will be forwarded to the *compiler* BCC32.EXE.

➔ Use the *MS-DOS editor* to create your actual source code. Create a file called NEW1.CPP for this in the C:\BCC55\IN directory using the editor and add the source code as described above. Save the file now.

➔ You are still in the C:\BCC55\IN directory. Now start the batch file just like any other program with the file name new1.cpp as the only parameter. Your program is now compiled and linked as a Windows program.

```
compile new1.cpp
```

➔ Now change to the C:\BCC55\OUT directory. This directory contains your completed program as an EXE file. Start it using the name new1.exe.

MS Visual C++ 6.0

It is much easier to write a Windows program using this graphic user interface. But it's no fun because personally I find it unclear and confusing. Of course, it is entirely up to you to decide which interface you want to use for programming. We will now create a program using this interface.

➔ Start *MS Visual C++ 6.0*.

➔ Select FILE/NEW. Click the PROJECTS tab and go to the Win32 Application list item, as shown in Figure 1.1.

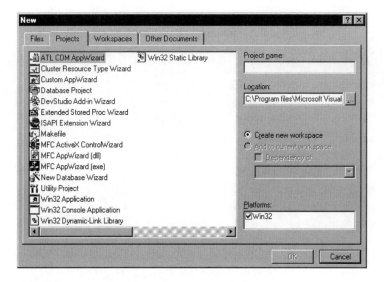

Figure 1.1 *Selecting the type of application*

→ Enter the project name *new1*. Click OK.

→ Select a simple *Win32 application*. Click Finish.

→ Click OK.

→ Select the FILES tab at the bottom left of the screen. Look for the file NEW1.CPP. When you double-click this file name, your source code file opens. Enter the source code here. There is no need to enter the *WinMain* lines again.

→ Start your source code by clicking the CREATE/RUN MENU item in NEW1.EXE.

→ Save your program using FILE/SAVE ALL or FILE/SAVE.

→ Exit *MS Visual C++ 6.0* by selecting FILE/EXIT.

→ Your program is stored in *MS Visual C++ 6.0* in the /Debug directory for your project.

1.2 The first application

1.2.1 *Off we go!*

In our first application, we want to generate a window. This window should appear on the screen and the user must be able to close it. Here is the source code for this application:

```
#include <windows.h>

LRESULT CALLBACK WndProc (HWND, UINT, WPARAM, LPARAM);

int APIENTRY WinMain(HINSTANCE hInstance,
                     HINSTANCE hPrevInstance,
                     LPSTR     lpCmdLine,
                     int       nCmdShow )
{
   WNDCLASS WndClass;
   WndClass.style = 0;
   WndClass.cbClsExtra = 0;
   WndClass.cbWndExtra = 0;
   WndClass.lpfnWndProc = WndProc;
   WndClass.hInstance = hInstance;
   WndClass.hbrBackground = (HBRUSH) (COLOR_WINDOW+1);
   WndClass.hCursor = 0;
   WndClass.hIcon = 0;
   WndClass.lpszMenuName = 0;
   WndClass.lpszClassName = "WinProg";

   RegisterClass(&WndClass);

   HWND hWindow;
   hWindow = CreateWindow("WinProg","Window",
                     WS_OVERLAPPEDWINDOW,
                     0,0,400,400,NULL,NULL,
                     hInstance, NULL);

   ShowWindow (hWindow, nCmdShow);

   UpdateWindow (hWindow);

   MSG Message;
   while (GetMessage(&Message, NULL, 0, 0))
   {
      DispatchMessage(&Message);
   }
   return (Message.wParam);
}
LRESULT CALLBACK WndProc (HWND hWnd, UINT uiMessage,
                          WPARAM wParam,LPARAM lParam)
```

```
{
   switch(uiMessage)
   {
      case WM_DESTROY:
         PostQuitMessage(0);
         return 0;
      default:
         return DefWindowProc (hWnd, uiMessage,
                               wParam, lParam);

   }
}
```

The application should look like Figure 1.2 after you start it.

Figure 1.2 *The application after you start it*

1.2.2   Explanation of the source code

You now know that this application displays a window. Users can close this window, thereby closing the application. We will now discuss exactly what happens.

Incorporating the WINDOWS.H file

This file contains references to other header files that are used to access the Windows functions, i.e. the API functions. The data type and structure definitions are also stored in these header files (or in references to other header files). Windows provides the API functions.

The prototype of a new function

This function is extremely important. At this point, we will only say that it is used later to allow the window to communicate with Windows.

The WinMain function

This is the entry-level function because the application's actual code begins here. All Windows programs use this function.

The window class

A structure of the type WNDCLASS is declared first. The structure determines the general properties of the windows that are created using this structure. It is called `WndClass`. The variables of the structure are explained in greater detail below:

```
typedef struct _WNDCLASS
{
    UINT    style;
    WNDPROC lpfnWndProc;
    int     cbClsExtra;
    int     cbWndExtra;
    HANDLE  hInstance;
    HICON   hIcon;
    HCURSOR hCursor;
    HBRUSH  hbrBackground;
    LPCTSTR lpszMenuName;
    LPCTSTR lpszClassName;
} WNDCLASS;
```

The WNDCLASS structure is declared as follows in the application:

```
WNDCLASS WndClass;
WndClass.cbClsExtra = 0;
WndClass.cbWndExtra = 0;
WndClass.lpfnWndProc = WndProc;
WndClass.hInstance = hInstance;
WndClass.hbrBackground = (HBRUSH) (COLOR_WINDOW+1);
WndClass.hCursor = 0;
WndClass.hIcon = 0;
WndClass.lpszMenuName = 0;
WndClass.lpszClassName = "WinProg";
```

You are probably surprised at the various types of variables. These types are defined in the Windows header files. They are simply different names for normal C++ variable types. For example, UINT is an unsigned int, WNDPROC is a pointer to a function, HANDLE, HCURSOR, HBRUSH are unsigned ints and LPCTSTR is a constant pointer of the type `char`.

The structure includes several variables:

→ The `style` variable defines the general appearance of the windows that are created using this structure.

→ `lpfnWndProc` is a pointer to a function, which the window uses to communicate with Windows.

→ `cbClsExtra` is not relevant because it relates to the allocation for additional bytes.

→ `cbWndExtra` is used for exactly the same purpose as `cbClsExtra`.

→ `hInstance` is very important. This parameter defines that all the generated windows belong to an application. Here, we come across the variable type HANDLE for the first time. Handles are extremely important for Windows programming. A handle is an `unsigned int` and serves as an index to a list. This list contains references to data structures that are part of the object. A function that creates an object returns a handle that identifies this object uniquely. This works in practice in the following way: we call the Windows function `CreateWindow`. This function creates a data structure, namely the object, which contains various properties of the window, e.g. from WNDCLASS. This structure must now be identified in the memory using an entry in a list. The function returns a handle. This is an index to this list. Here, we are asked for a handle that identifies our program.

→ `hIcon` and `hCursor` are also handles to Icon and Cursor objects.

→ `hBrush` is the handle to an object containing a fill pattern. In this case, the handle of the `COLOR_WINDOW` object is used.

→ `lpszMenuName` is a constant pointer to a `char` array, i.e. a character string. Since we don't need a menu, this value is set to 0.

→ `lpszClassName` is the name of the data structure that is created. This variable is a constant pointer to a `char` array. All pointers to `char` arrays in Windows must be null-terminated. This means that they must end with a null value. ANSI character strings are used primarily throughout this manual. For more information on UNICODE, please refer to the later chapters. This data structure is used later to create objects. It is therefore a class because the data structure contains data and function definitions. It is for this reason that this data structure is also called window class.

What is the actual significance of having a handle? There are data structures in the memory, e.g. the data structures of a window. There are functions for these data structures and these functions are grouped together in one object. The description of which function belongs to which data structure is therefore a class. So, there are window classes and window objects. The window objects are accessed using handles. In other words, a handle is an index to a list. The index can be used to access data contained in the object. This data is accessed using functions for the objects. The handle is passed to the functions, which work only with one specific object and modify the data contained in one object.

As mentioned earlier, we will now register the WNDCLASS structure with Windows. This means that Windows is informed of the existence of this class so that you can create windows using this class with other Windows functions. The function is called RegisterClass.

```
ATOM RegisterClass (CONST WNDCLASS *lpWndClass);
```

You can call the function as follows:

```
RegisterClass(&WndClass)
```

The function requests the pointer to the structure and supplies a return value. This return value is null if the function fails. Otherwise, we are not particularly interested in the return value at present.

Creating the window

The next step is to create the window. You can use the CreateWindow function for this. You must first declare a variable however. This variable must be of the type HWND. This type, in turn, is a handle for a window:

```
HWND hWindow;
```

This calls the CreateWindow function. It creates a data structure for the window, i.e. the object. This data structure knows which application created the window and which function is to be called to communicate with Windows, for example. The CreateWindow function also defines the specific properties of the window, which are added to the window class properties. Each window can only be created by one window class:

```
HWND CreateWindow(LPCTSTR lpClassName,
                  LPCTSTR lpWindowName,
                  DWORD dwStyle,
                  int x,
                  int y,
                  int nWidth,
                  int nHeight,
                  HWND hWndParent,
                  HMENU hMenu,
                  HANDLE hInstance,
```

```
            LPVOID lpParam
);
```

The call is displayed again:

```
hWindow = CreateWindow("WinProg","Window",
                       WS_OVERLAPPEDWINDOW,
                       0,0,400,400,NULL,NULL,
                       hInstance, NULL);
```

We will now look at the individual function parameters:

→ The lpClassName function parameter is a constant pointer to a char array. This string contains the name of the window class to be used to create the window object. The window class does not indicate whether a window belongs to an application.

→ The lpWindowName function parameter is also a constant pointer to a char array. It contains a string that gives the window a name. This name is displayed in the title bar of the window.

→ dwStyles contains other specific properties of the window. In this case, the property is WS_OVERLAPPEDWINDOW. A number of properties can be specified. These are then linked using a logical or. This could look like this in practice: WS_Property1 | WS_Property2. Both values are constants. The bits in these constants are chosen in such a way that only one single bit is set to 1. The logical or of two constants would therefore set various bits that are evaluated by the function. This principle applies to many Windows functions that use this type of property.

→ x, y, nWidth, and nHeight are the position and size of the window, where x and y indicate the top left position of the window in relation to its parent. This value is calculated in pixels. The value of the top left corner is x=0 and y=0. nWidth and nHeight indicate the width and height of the window.

→ hWndParent is the handle of the parent window. If 0 appears here, the window does not have a parent window.

→ hMenu is a handle to a window menu. Since we don't need a menu at present, the value is set to 0.

→ hInstance is the handle to our application. This handle is passed on from the WinMain function. Even our application is assigned a Windows handle at the start. Since there are also functions for the data structure of your application, which comprises not only code, but also other information, your application can also be regarded as an object. As a result, the window is assigned uniquely to the application.

→ The lParam parameter is used for processing messages in Windows. Message processing is described in more detail later.

Displaying the window

We now have to display the window. You can use the `ShowWindow` function for this:

```
BOOL ShowWindow (HWND hWnd,int nCmdShow);
```

And now to use this in the sample program:

```
ShowWindow (hWindow, nCmdShow);
```

➜ The first function parameter `hWnd` is the handle of the window, which we want to display.

➜ `nCmdShow` is an `int` value, which specifies various display properties. We will use the display mode supplied by the `WinMain` function for our window.

This command only displays the window managed by Windows, with its various properties. But we also want to display the contents. We use the term contents to describe the white area that you can see in the window. You can use the `UpdateWindow` function to display the contents:

```
BOOL UpdateWindow ( HWND hWnd);
```

The function looks like this in the sample program:

```
UpdateWindow (hWindow);
```

➜ The first and only function parameter is the handle of the window whose contents is to be displayed.

The message loop

The *message loop* is one of the main components of Windows applications. It is important to understand how Windows actually works. Applications in Windows are no longer run in the same way as DOS applications. This means that their actual code is no longer executed in a specific sequence. Given that Windows is a multitasking operating system, it should be possible to run a number of applications at the same time. This is not the case, however, because a computer normally has only one processor. Of course, this can only execute one code. But Windows uses a special technique to give the impression that all the applications are running side-by-side. This involves switching back and forth between the various code elements and executing each code for a certain length of time. Another special feature is that every application in Windows is assigned a queue. This is simply a list in which messages are entered. For example, these messages can be mouse clicks, window movements, etc. The whole operation runs as follows: Windows determines a mouse click in a window. It then sends a message to the queue belonging to the corresponding application. This message contains the handle of the window in which the mouse click was detected, the coordinates of the click, the buttons, and other information. At this point, the *message loop* comes into play. The term *message loop* refers to the `while` loop that follows in the sample application. The task of the message loop is to process messages. The system, the application, or other applications send messages to windows. The message principle is designed to enable a number of applications running side-by-side to be displayed graphically on the screen. The windows therefore send messages to each other in order to let another window know that it must redraw itself. If this principle were not implemented, either only one application could be displayed on the screen at any one time, or the applications would display continually at the same position in the graphics memory.

```
MSG Message;
while (GetMessage(&Message, NULL, 0, 0))
{
    DispatchMessage(&Message);
}
```

This loop can also occur in another form with the following functions. The `Get-Message` function gets a message from the application's queue. If the message WM_QUIT appears here, `GetMessage` returns the value 0 and the application is terminated because the program has reached the end of its code. The message is stored in a message structure. This structure is called Message here. `Dispatch-Message` forwards this message structure to the window's function. This means the following for the window in the sample application: The function for message processing was defined in the window class. `DispatchMessage` determines the function from the data structure of the window object and presents it with the message for processing. The continuation of the program code therefore begins with the function that was specified in the window class. The exact function syntax is given below:

```
BOOL GetMessage( LPMSG lpMsg, HWND hWnd,
                 UINT wMsgFilterMin, UINT wMsgFilterMax);
LONG DispatchMessage( CONST MSG *lpmsg);
```

The functions were used as follows in the sample application:

```
GetMessage(&Message, NULL, 0, 0))
DispatchMessage(&Message);
```

We will first discuss `GetMessage`:

➜ The first function parameter `lpMsg` requests a pointer to a message structure. The LPMSG variable type is nothing other than a pointer to an MSG structure.

➜ The second function parameter specifies the handle of the window from which the messages are to be processed. The value 0 means that all the messages are processed. You see from this that only windows can actually receive messages.

→ You can use the `wMsgFilterMin` and `wMsgFilterMax` function parameters to set the range of the messages that are to be returned. These values are set to 0 so that all the messages are returned.

→ The `return value` of the function is 0 for the WM_QUIT message and is not equal to 0 for the other messages. All messages are indicated by WM. This message is represented by constant values.

We will now look at the message parameter used in `DispatchMessage`.

→ This function requests a single parameter in the form of the pointer to the message structure, which is to be passed to the function to be called.

The message structure looks like this:

```
typedef struct tagMSG
{
    HWND    hwnd;
    UINT    message;
    WPARAM  wParam;
    LPARAM  lParam;
    DWORD   time;
    POINT   pt;
} MSG;
```

This structure contains a number of variables:

```
MSG Message
```

Each of the variables is explained below:

→ hwnd contains the handle of the window for which the message is intended.

→ message contains the value of the message. This value is one of the constants in the form WM_CREATE, WM_SETTEXT, etc.

→ wParam is the first function parameter.

→ lParam is the second function parameter.

→ time contains the time at which the message was created.

→ pt is another structure:

```
typedef struct tagPOINT
{   LONG x;
    LONG y;
} POINT;
```

The two variables of the structure x,y contain the position of the cursor on the screen.

The return value from the application

The application supplies a return value. This return value is transferred from the parameter in the WM_QUIT message.

The message processing function

A window needs a function in order to process the messages that are sent to the window. The following prototype of the function is intended as a starting point:

```
LRESULT CALLBACK WndProc (HWND, UINT, WPARAM, LPARAM);
```

The function parameters are filled with the message.

→ The first parameter is the handle of the window to which the message is going.
→ The second parameter determines the message.
→ The third and fourth parameters are simply additional information or parameters of the message.
→ The return value of this function is supplied by Dispatch Message.

The messages are processed in this function. This is done using switch branching:

```
switch(uiMessage)
{
    case WM_DESTROY:
        PostQuitMessage(0);
        return 0;
    default:
        return DefWindowProc (hWnd, uiMessage,
                              wParam, lParam);
}
```

The only message that is evaluated by the sample program is WM_DESTROY. When this function is sent, the PostQuitMessage function is called. This function sends the WM_QUIT message to its own queue, thereby quitting the program. The WM_DESTROY message is triggered when the window is closed. Otherwise, the DefWindowProc function is called and this in turn triggers a standard function for the message.

```
VOID PostQuitMessage( int nExitCode);
LRESULT DefWindowProc( HWND hWnd, UINT Msg,
                       WPARAM wParam, LPARAM lParam);
```

We have already shown how the functions are used. We will now move on to describe the parameters used in PostQuitMessage:

→ nExitCode specifies the value for wParam in WM_QUIT.

The parameters used in `DefWindowProc` are as follows:

→ All the message parameters, which were also passed to the `WndProc` function, are simply transferred to this function.

1.3 General information on objects

Objects are the main components of Windows programming. They are not C++ objects, but data structures in the memory. For the various data structures, there are certain functions that are used to meet the conditions for an object. For example, a window object can only be processed using functions for a window object. An example of such a function would be `SetWindowPos`. The functions expect a handle. This handle is an index to a list. The functions need this index in order to process the data structure. All the objects that were created should be deleted when you exit a program.

1.4 Note

Objects should always be removed from memory at the end of the program. You can do this using corresponding functions, which can be found in the SDK.

We don't always do this in this manual, but the only reason for this is so that we can concentrate on the most important aspects of programming. The programmer can add these code sections later.

Introduction to the GDI

2.1 What is the GDI?

The GDI is a subgrouping of the Win32 API. The Win32 API describes all the functions for the Windows 32-bit operating system. API stands for *Application Programming Interface*.

Which specific functions are actually available on the GDI? The abbreviation GDI stands for *Graphics Device Interface*. It includes the functions that allow you to draw and write in a window, i.e. the functions for displaying graphics in windows. However, the GDI functions are not only used on graphics areas in windows. Instead, they are a set of functions that allow you to display graphics using a device context[1] object. This device context object does not allow complete access to the graphics memory – in other words: the GDI functions are almost only used on the area that appeared white in the window in the last application. This area is called the client area of a window. This area has its own device context object, which is specified in the window object. The `BeginPaint` and `GetDC` functions allow you to obtain a handle to the device context. In the case of a window, this relates to a screen dump in the window, but can refer equally to a printout. To sum up: the GDI includes all the functions that allow you to access the device context. This does not have to involve accessing the graphics memory, but can also involve accessing the output. This allows you to use all the functions of the GDI both for displaying and printing graphics. The GDI functions are also used in connection with other devices that have something to do with graphics. The disadvantage of the GDI is that the graphics memory cannot be changed directly, but only using GDI functions.

---

1. We should first explain the term 'device context'. Almost all the functions of the GDI use a device context object. This object refers to part of the screen memory. This part of the memory is called the device context. The GDI functions then draw in this device context. Every window has a device context object, but in this case, the device context is restricted only to the contents of the window. It does not include the frame and title bar, for example.

Once you have determined the handle for a device context object, you can release it again using the `EndPaint` and `ReleaseDC` functions.

The next application shows how to use the GDI. Various graphics functions will be used in this application. It is slightly more difficult to display text, so we will not discuss this at this point. The use of the graphics functions involves a number of objects, which we must create first. For example, we must first provide a Pen, i.e. a Pen object, for a line. This object then contains information about the width, type and color of the line. Please note at this point that these objects are not objects in the C++ sense, but Windows-specific objects. They are therefore called objects because a data structure that can be accessed using handles exists in the memory. Furthermore, there are functions available for these data structures: this makes it an object. You can only access these objects using the Win32 API.

2.2 The GDI program

2.2.1   The source code

This application is designed to provide an introduction to the GDI functions. The GDI functions for drawing, in particular, are described here. Figure 2.1 shows the application after you have started it.

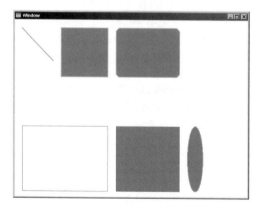

Figure 2.1 *Sample application with GDI drawing functions after you start it*

```
#include <windows.h>

LRESULT CALLBACK WndProc (HWND, UINT, WPARAM, LPARAM);

int APIENTRY WinMain(HINSTANCE hInstance,
```

```
                    HINSTANCE hPrevInstance,
                    LPSTR     lpCmdLine,
                    int       nCmdShow )
{
   WNDCLASS WndClass;
   WndClass.style = 0;
   WndClass.cbClsExtra = 0;
   WndClass.cbWndExtra = 0;
   WndClass.lpfnWndProc = WndProc;
   WndClass.hInstance = hInstance;
   WndClass.hbrBackground = (HBRUSH) (COLOR_WINDOW+1);
   WndClass.hCursor = LoadCursor (NULL, IDC_ARROW);
   WndClass.hIcon = LoadIcon (NULL, IDI_APPLICATION);
   WndClass.lpszMenuName = 0;
   WndClass.lpszClassName = "WinProg";

   RegisterClass(&WndClass);

   HWND hWindow;
   hWindow = CreateWindow("WinProg","Window",
                    WS_OVERLAPPEDWINDOW,
                    0,0,600,460,NULL,NULL,
                    hInstance, NULL);

   ShowWindow (hWindow, nCmdShow);

   UpdateWindow (hWindow);

   MSG Message;
   while (GetMessage(&Message, NULL, 0, 0))
   {
      DispatchMessage(&Message);
   }
   return (Message.wParam);
}

LRESULT CALLBACK WndProc (HWND hWnd, UINT uiMessage,
                    WPARAM wParam,LPARAM lParam)
{
   switch(uiMessage)
   {
      case WM_PAINT:
```

```
            HPEN hPen;
            HPEN hPenalt;
            HBRUSH hBrush;
            HBRUSH hBrushalt;
            hBrush = CreateSolidBrush (RGB(255,100,0));
            hPen = CreatePen (PS_SOLID,2,RGB(0,255,255));
            HDC hdc;
            PAINTSTRUCT ps;
            hdc = BeginPaint (hWnd, &ps);
            hBrushalt = SelectObject (hdc, hBrush);
            hPenalt = SelectObject (hdc, hPen);
            MoveToEx (hdc, 20, 20, NULL);
            LineTo (hdc, 100, 100);
            Rectangle (hdc, 120, 20, 240, 140);
            RoundRect (hdc, 260, 20, 420, 140, 20, 20);

            RECT rect;
            SetRect (&rect, 20, 260, 240, 420);
            FrameRect (hdc, &rect, hBrush);
            SetRect (&rect, 260, 260, 420, 420);
            FillRect (hdc, &rect, hBrush);
            Ellipse (hdc, 440, 260, 480, 420);
            SelectObject (hdc, hBrushalt);
            SelectObject (hdc, hPenalt);
            DeleteObject (hPen);
            DeleteObject (hBrush);
            EndPaint (hWnd, &ps);
            return 0;
        case WM_DESTROY:
            PostQuitMessage(0);
            return 0;
        default:
            return DefWindowProc (hWnd, uiMessage,
                                    wParam, lParam);
    }
}
```

2.2.2   Explanation of the source code

Cursor and icon

The structure of the source code is the same as in the first sample application. The first change involves the declaration of the variables of the WNDCLASS structure. The Hcursor variable is assigned a handle. The LoadCursor function links the Cursor object to a predefined Windows cursor. The LoadIcon function works in the same way. It links a predefined icon to an Icon object. The handle of the Icon object is then supplied as a return value in the same way as the handle of the Cursor object. We will now look at the LoadCursor function:

```
HCURSOR LoadCursor( HINSTANCE hInstance,
                    LPCTSTR lpCursorName);
```

This function is used in the source code in the following way:

```
WndClass.hCursor = LoadCursor (NULL, IDC_ARROW);
```

The following function parameters are used:

→ hInstance is set to NULL in order to load a predefined cursor.
→ lpCursorName contains the identifier for the predefined cursor.
→ The handle of the object, to which the predefined cursor is linked, is supplied as the return value.

Now, let's look at the LoadIcon function:

```
HICON LoadIcon( HINSTANCE hInstance, LPCTSTR lpIconName);
```

This function is used in the source code in the following way:

```
WndClass.hIcon = LoadIcon (NULL, IDI_APPLICATION);
```

The function parameters are explained below:

→ hInstance is set to NULL in order to use a predefined icon.
→ lpIconName contains the identifier for the predefined icon.
→ The function supplies the handle of the Icon object, which is linked to the icon, as the return value.

The two functions in the WNDCLASS structure ensure that the cursor appears as an arrow in the window area. The window also has an icon straight away.

Other changes to the message loop

Other changes include the modified width and height of the window. All in all, the window has become slightly bigger.

Changes in the WndProc function

The most important change in `WndProc` is the way in which the WM_PAINT message is handled. Parts of the window's device context can become invalid if they are overlapped by another window, for example. The title bars and the frame of the window are redrawn automatically by `DefWindowProc`. If part of the device context is changed on the screen, however, this triggers a WM_PAINT message. This message is sent to the corresponding window function via `DispatchMessage`, or the `WndProc` function is called using the WM_PAINT message. The `BeginPaint` function fills the invalid area of the device context using `hBrush` in `WndClass.hbrBackground`. Lines are then drawn on the device context using graphics functions, such as `LineTo`. And finally, the device context of the window determined by `BeginPaint` must be released again.

Creating the individual property objects for the drawing functions

The first step is to create objects for the device context of the window. The individual drawing functions for the window use these objects. This involves using the `CreateSolidBrush` and `CreatePen` functions, in particular. `CreateSolidBrush` creates a fill pattern object and `CreatePen` creates a drawing pen object. You must first declare two handles for this. These handles are of the variable type HBRUSH and HPEN. They point indirectly to the data structure of the list using an index in a list.

You need to use the `CreateSolidBrush` function to create a Brush object:

```
HBRUSH CreateSolidBrush( COLORREF crColor);
```

This function is used in the following way in the source code:

```
hBrush = CreateSolidBrush (RGB(255,100,0));
```

The function parameter is as follows:

➔ `crColor` is a function parameter of the variable type COLORREF. This variable type is a 32-bit value and specifies the value of an RGB color. An RGB color is made up of three color components: red, green and blue. They have values between 0 and 255 and since they each require only one byte, they are all stored in a 32-bit value. This value is of the type COLORREF and is created by the RGB macro. You can also specify this value manually by entering the individual bytes in hexadecimal form. 0x000000ff is an example for the color Blue. The three smallest bytes of the 32-bit value are always used.

➔ The function supplies a handle to a new Brush object as the `return value`.

➔ The RGB macro creates the COLORREF value from red, green and blue color components.

```
COLORREF RGB( BYTE bRed, BYTE bGreen, BYTE bBlue);
```

The call is issued – as described above – in the `CreateSolidBrush` function. We will now look at the parameters for this macro:

→ All three parameters are of the type BYTE, i.e. 8-bit unsigned variables. They can have values from 0 through 255. Each parameter specifies the value of the color component for the color. The first stands for red, the second for green and the third for blue.

Now, let's talk about the `CreatePen` function. It creates a Pen object. It contains data for various drawing functions. This value is generally used for lines:

```
HPEN CreatePen( int fnPenStyle, int nWidth,
                COLORREF crColor);
```

This function is used in the following way in the source code:

```
hPen = CreatePen (PS_SOLID,2,RGB(0,255,255));
```

The function parameters are discussed below:

→ `fnPenStyle` indicates the type of line. The line can be continuous, broken, etc. The value PS_SOLID specifies a continuous line. Here, we simply use predefined values to which the function reacts accordingly.

→ `nWidth` specifies the width of the line that is drawn using this object.

→ `crColor` is again a value of the variable type COLORREF. This means that an RGB color is expected. The line that is drawn using this Pen object appears in this color. Of course, this value is also created using the RGB macro.

The BeginPaint and EndPaint functions

Both functions are very important. `BeginPaint` initiates a number of different actions. When you call this function, the invalid part of the window is filled using the window's `hbrBackground` Brush object. This object was specified in WND-CLASS. It was a predefined Windows Brush object. The invalid area is then declared valid. Values are also returned in a structure of the type PAINTSTRUCT. This structure contains information about the invalid rectangle or box. The function supplies the handle to a device context object as the `return value`. All the GDI functions need this value because lines can only be drawn to this object. `Begin-Paint` must be included in the WM_PAINT function because it declares the invalid box valid again. An invalid box always relates to a device context object. If a WM_PAINT message is processed and removed from the application's queue, but the invalid box is not declared valid, a WM_PAINT message will appear again in the queue. If such a message already exists and you want to send another WM_PAINT message to the window, the two messages are first combined to form one message. The description of the invalid boxes appears in the window object. This description is extended. In conclusion, we must point out that every handle to a device context object must be released again by the EndPaint function so that you can continue to access the device context object. Now, let's move on to the function syntax:

```
HDC BeginPaint( HWND hwnd, LPPAINTSTRUCT lpPaint);
```

This looks like this in the source code:

```
hdc = BeginPaint (hWnd, &ps);
```

The function parameters are as follows:

→ hwnd specifies the handle to the window object, which contains the device context object in which the drawing is to be done.

→ lpPaint must be a pointer to a structure of the type PAINTSTRUCT. This structure is filled with details of the invalid box.

→ A handle to the device context object is supplied as the return value. This handle is used to draw in the device context object using GDI functions.

The PAINTSTRUCT structure is as follows:

```
typedef struct tagPAINTSTRUCT
{
    HDC  hdc;
    BOOL fErase;
    RECT rcPaint;
    BOOL fRestore;
    BOOL fIncUpdate;
    BYTE rgbReserved[32];
} PAINTSTRUCT;
```

and contains the following variables:

→ hdc is assigned the handle to the device context object. This is the same handle that is returned by BeginPaint.

→ fErase is NULL if the area of the invalid box was redrawn using hbrBackground from WNDCLASS. We will discuss later a case in which this value is TRUE, but this is not relevant here.

→ rcPaint is a structure of the type RECT. It contains the data for the invalid box.

→ The other three function parameters are used internally by the system.

The new RECT structure:

```
typedef struct _RECT
{
    LONG left;
    LONG top;
```

```
    LONG right;
    LONG bottom;
} RECT;
```

The individual variables of the structure are explained below:

→ All four variables are of the type LONG. This is a 32-bit signed integer. left and top specify the top left corner of the box in pixels. These values are based on the distance from the top left corner of the device context. The variables right and bottom are also based on the distance to the top left corner of the device context and specify the bottom right corner of the box in pixels.

The SelectObject function

The SelectObject function assigns an object to a device context. This object is then linked to the device context. All the functions that use the device context are based on objects that are linked to this.

```
HGDIOBJ SelectObject( HDC hdc, HGDIOBJ hgdiobj);
```

This function is needed twice in the source code of the sample application:

```
SelectObject (hdc, hBrush);
SelectObject (hdc, hPen);
```

The function parameters are explained below:

→ hdc requests the handle to a device context object.
→ hgdiobj requests the handle to a GDI object. This can be Brush or Pen objects, for example. The device context object then points to the GDI objects that were assigned to the device context.
→ The function supplies the handle to the previous GDI object, which was linked to the device context, as the return value. If the function fails, it returns the value NULL.

Simple GDI drawing functions

We call functions with only a few parameters "simple GDI drawing functions". These functions do not use any arrays either. They are used to draw basic geometric shapes. Simple GDI drawing functions include the functions described below.

The MoveToEx function does not draw anything, but defines the position of a drawing cursor on the device context, i.e. a position on the device context, which is used by other functions. The function syntax is as follows:

```
BOOL MoveToEx( HDC hdc, int X, int Y, LPPOINT lpPoint);
```

This function is used in the following way in the source code:

```
MoveToEx (hdc, 20, 20, NULL);
```

The function parameters are explained below:

→ hdc defines the device context to be used to set the value of this position.

→ X, Y define the position. Both parameters relate to the top left corner. The distance from this corner is specified. The pixel value in the top left corner is 0,0.

→ lpPoint expects the pointer to a structure of the type POINT. The data for the previous position is then stored in this structure. (The Point structure was discussed earlier in Chapter 1.)

→ The function supplies the value 0 as the return value in the event of an error. Otherwise, the return value is not equal to 0.

The next function is LineTo. It draws a line into the device context using the data specified for the Pen object. The line begins at the position defined by the MoveTo function and ends at the parameters defined in LineTo. The syntax of the function is as follows:

```
BOOL LineTo( HDC hdc, int nXEnd, int nYEnd);
```

This function is used in the following way in the source code:

```
LineTo (hdc, 100, 100);
```

Now, let's look at the individual parameters:

→ The hdc parameter specifies the handle to a device context.

→ nXEnd, nYEnd specify the position in the device context, measured from the top left corner.

Yet another function is Rectangle. This function draws a rectangle or box. The box is framed with the properties specified in the Pen object and filled with the properties specified in the Brush object. The function syntax is described below.

```
BOOL Rectangle( HDC hdc, int nLeftRect, int nTopRect,
                int nRightRect, int nBottomRect);
```

This function is used in the following way in the source code:

```
Rectangle (hdc, 120, 20, 240, 140);
```

The function parameters are as follows:

→ hdc is the handle to a device context.

→ nLeftRect, nTopRect, nRightRect, nBottomRect specify the position of the box in the device context. In other words: the position of the box in the memory of the screen to which the device context object refers. The device context is therefore the memory of a device to which the device context object refers. All values are specified in pixels.

The next function is `RoundRect`. This function is almost identical to `Rectangle`, but has two more parameters. It fills a box with rounded corners with the properties in the Brush object. The frame is drawn using the properties in the Pen object.

```
BOOL RoundRect( HDC hdc, int nLeftRect, int nTopRect,
                int nRightRect, int nBottomRect,
                int nWidth, int nHeight);
```

This function looks like this in the source code:

```
RoundRect (hdc, 260, 20, 420, 140, 20, 20);
```

The individual parameters are as follows:

→ hdc specifies the handle to the device context object.
→ nLeftRect, nTopRect, nRightRect, nBottomRect specify the position of the box in pixels, as for `Rectangle`.
→ nWidth, nHeight set the width and height of the ellipse, which is used to round the corners of the box.

The next function does not draw in a device context, i.e. in a memory area on the screen, but relates to the RECT structure, which we discussed earlier. It fills the variables of the RECT structure with the specified parameters so that you don't have to assign these manually:

```
BOOL SetRect( LPRECT lprc, int xLeft, int yTop,
              int xRight, int yBottom);
```

This function is used in the following way in the source code:

```
SetRect (&rect, 20, 260, 240, 420);
```

It includes the following parameters:

→ lprc requests the pointer to a RECT structure.
→ The following four parameters are assigned to this RECT structure.

The `FrameRect` function uses a structure of the type RECT to draw an empty box with only a frame. The properties of the frame are specified using a Brush object:

```
int FrameRect( HDC hDC, CONST RECT *lprc, HBRUSH hbr);
```

The function looks like this in the source code:

```
FrameRect (hdc, &rect, hBrush);
```

Where the parameters are as follows:

→ hDC specifies the handle to the device context object.
→ lprc requests a pointer to a RECT structure.

➡ hbr specifies a separate Brush object, which uses this function for drawing. The Brush object of the device context object is not used.

The next function is called FillRect. It has the same parameters as Frame-Rect and works in the same way. The only difference is that this function fills the specified box:

```
int FillRect( HDC hDC, CONST RECT *lprc, HBRUSH hbr);
```

This function is used in the following way in the source code:

```
FillRect (hdc, &rect, hBrush);
```

The function parameters are as follows:

➡ hDC is the handle to the device context object.
➡ lprc is a pointer to a RECT structure.
➡ hbr is the handle to a Brush object, which is to use this function for drawing.

Ellipse is yet another function – and this is the last function presented in this manual. It draws an ellipse on the device context. The Pen object specifies the frame of the ellipse and the Brush object of the device context object specifies how the object is filled.

```
BOOL Ellipse( HDC hdc, int nLeftRect, int nTopRect,
              int nRightRect, int nBottomRect);
```

This function is used in the following way in the source code:

```
Ellipse (hdc, 440, 260, 480, 420);
```

The function parameters are as follows:

➡ hdc specifies the handle to the device context object.
➡ nLeftRect, nTopRect, nRightRect and nBottomRect specify a rectangular area of the device context, in which the ellipse is drawn.

Deleting Pen and Brush objects

After you have used the Pen and Brush objects you created to complete your drawing, you must delete these from the memory. The old Pen and Brush objects then have to be restored.

```
        DeleteObject (hPen);
        DeleteObject (hBrush);
```

This is necessary if the objects are created again and again. If you want to retain the link between a device context and an object, you obviously should not delete this object.

EndPaint

The `EndPaint` function releases the device context object again:

```
EndPaint (hWnd, &ps);
```

A device context should always be released again as soon as the drawing is completed.

Displaying text using the GDI

3.1 General information

Everything in this chapter centers on displaying text using the GDI. However, we will first provide you with some fundamental information on this. The keyboard returns scan codes. These scan codes identify each key uniquely. The problem we have now involves assigning another code, which is country-specific and specifies a character, to these scan codes. For this purpose, we have character sets, which assign values to characters. These codes are often different for specific countries. The standard is the ISO standard. It covers the codes from 0x20 through 0x7F. The ASCII code includes this ISO standard and defines the lower values from 0x00 through 0x19. The extended ASCII code also defines the upper 128 values. These values cover block graphics. The extended ASCII code is also called the OEM character set. Windows does not actually use any of these character sets, but a new standard was defined specifically for Windows. This new character set is called ANSI. It includes the ISO standard character set, i.e. the definition of 0x20 through 0x7F. There are a number of variants of ANSI that relate to the changes above 0x7F through 0xFF. The codes from 0x00 through 0x1F are not defined. The Western European ANSI version is also called ISO 8859. Compilers like C and C++ need the source code, which is based on this character set. This means that you must write the functions using this character set.

There are two different types of fonts in Windows: GDI fonts and TrueType fonts. The GDI fonts are bitmap fonts. A raster with a set bit and a non-set bit is simply transferred to the output medium. You cannot modify the size of these fonts very well, but you can use them very quickly for graphics applications. They can contain a number of country-specific character sets and are stored in files with the extension FONT. There are proportional and non-proportional fonts there. TrueType fonts, on the other hand, are vector fonts. They contain pixel coordinates that are linked by lines. They are therefore ideally suited for being displayed in various sizes. Given that they must be recalculated every time, however, they are not very suitable for fast graphic displays. The TrueType fonts also contain a number of country-specific character sets.

This chapter describes how to use the bitmap fonts.

3.2 Creating text using the GDI

3.2.1 The source code

The next application is an example of how to use fonts. No TrueType fonts are used here, instead we use various standard Windows character sets. Figure 3.1 shows the application after you have started it.

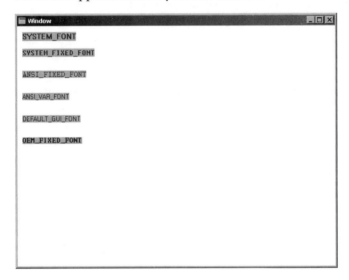

Figure 3.1 *Fonts after you start the application*

```
#include <windows.h>

LRESULT CALLBACK WndProc (HWND, UINT, WPARAM, LPARAM);

int APIENTRY WinMain(HINSTANCE hInstance,
                     HINSTANCE hPrevInstance,
                     LPSTR     lpCmdLine,
                     int       nCmdShow )
{
   WNDCLASS WndClass;
   WndClass.style = 0;
```

```
WndClass.cbClsExtra = 0;
WndClass.cbWndExtra = 0;
WndClass.lpfnWndProc = WndProc;
WndClass.hInstance = hInstance;
WndClass.hbrBackground = (HBRUSH) (COLOR_WINDOW+1);
WndClass.hCursor = LoadCursor (NULL, IDC_ARROW);
WndClass.hIcon = LoadIcon (NULL, IDI_APPLICATION);
WndClass.lpszMenuName = 0;
WndClass.lpszClassName = "WinProg";

RegisterClass(&WndClass);

HWND hWindow;
hWindow = CreateWindow("WinProg","Window",
                       WS_OVERLAPPEDWINDOW,
                       0,0,600,460,NULL,NULL,
                       hInstance, NULL);

ShowWindow (hWindow, nCmdShow);

UpdateWindow (hWindow);

MSG Message;
while (GetMessage(&Message, NULL, 0, 0))
{
   DispatchMessage(&Message);
}


   return (Message.wParam);
}

LRESULT CALLBACK WndProc (HWND hWnd, UINT uiMessage,
                          WPARAM wParam,LPARAM lParam)
{
   switch(uiMessage)
   {
      case WM_PAINT:
         HDC hdc;
         PAINTSTRUCT ps;
         hdc = BeginPaint (hWnd, &ps);
```

```
HFONT hFont;

hFont = (HFONT) GetStockObject ( SYSTEM_FONT);
SelectObject (hdc, hFont);
SetTextColor (hdc, RGB(0,0,180));
SetBkColor (hdc, RGB(190,180,200));
SetTextAlign (hdc, TA_LEFT);
char *string1;
string1 = new char[12];
lstrcpy (string1,"SYSTEM_FONT");
TextOut (hdc, 10, 10, string1, lstrlen(string1));

hFont =
     (HFONT) GetStockObject (SYSTEM_FIXED_FONT);
SelectObject (hdc, hFont);
delete (string1);
string1 = new char[80];
lstrcpy (string1,"SYSTEM_FIXED_FONT");
TextOut (hdc, 10, 40, string1, lstrlen(string1));

hFont = (HFONT) GetStockObject (ANSI_FIXED_FONT);
SelectObject (hdc, hFont);
delete (string1);
string1 = new char[80];

lstrcpy (string1,"ANSI_FIXED_FONT");
TextOut (hdc, 10, 80, string1, lstrlen(string1));

hFont = (HFONT) GetStockObject ( ANSI_VAR_FONT);
SelectObject (hdc, hFont);
delete (string1);
string1 = new char[80];
lstrcpy (string1,"ANSI_VAR_FONT");
TextOut (hdc, 10, 120, string1,
          lstrlen(string1));

hFont =
     (HFONT) GetStockObject ( DEFAULT_GUI_FONT);
SelectObject (hdc, hFont);
delete (string1);
string1 = new char[80];
lstrcpy (string1,"DEFAULT_GUI_FONT");
```

```
        TextOut (hdc, 10, 160, string1,
                 lstrlen(string1));

        hFont = (HFONT) GetStockObject ( OEM_FIXED_FONT);
        SelectObject (hdc, hFont);
        delete (string1);
        string1 = new char[80];
        lstrcpy (string1,"OEM_FIXED_FONT");
        TextOut (hdc, 10, 200, string1,
                 lstrlen(string1));

        EndPaint (hWnd, &ps);
        return 0;
    case WM_DESTROY:
        PostQuitMessage(0);
        return 0;
    default:
        return DefWindowProc (hWnd, uiMessage,
                              wParam, lParam);
    }
}
```

3.2.2   Explanation of the source code

The source code is based on the basic framework of the first application. Unlike the second source code, the differences relate only to the WM_PAINT area.

A new handle

The first change in the source code is in the word HFONT. This word declares a variable of the type HFONT. This is a handle to a font, i.e. a character set. Even the fonts are objects.

Getting the handle to a predefined font

You can use the GetStockObject function to get the handle to a predefined font. You must specify this font using a constant. The function then returns a handle to the font object. Since this function is capable of more than that, you must convert a general GDI handle value to a handle for a font. The function syntax is given below:

```
HGDIOBJ GetStockObject( int fnObject);
```

This function appears six times altogether. Each time, it gets the handle for a different font:

```
hFont = (HFONT) GetStockObject ( SYSTEM_FONT);
hFont = (HFONT) GetStockObject ( SYSTEM_FIXED_FONT);
hFont = (HFONT) GetStockObject ( ANSI_FIXED_FONT);
hFont = (HFONT) GetStockObject ( ANSI_VAR_FONT);
hFont = (HFONT) GetStockObject ( DEFAULT_GUI_FONT);
hFont = (HFONT) GetStockObject ( OEM_FIXED_FONT);
```

The function parameter is explained below:

→ `fnObject` specifies a constant. A handle to a different object is returned, depending on the constant.

→ The handle to an object, which was specified by the constant, is supplied as the `return value`. This is a general handle however. It still has to be converted.

Assigning the font to the device context

The handle of the font object is assigned to the device context object. This means that a reference is set from the device context object to the font object. The `SelectObject` function is used for this purpose. This function is linked with many GDI objects. You supply the function with the appropriate handle to the object, and it does all the rest. Since we discussed this function already in Chapter 2, we will not go into it in any detail here.

The font color

The device context object stores two properties for the color of the font. You can define the two values of the device context object using the functions `SetTextColor` and `SetBkColor`. The value you define using `SetTextColor` is used as the foreground color in the text output function `TextOut`. The value you set using `SetBkColor`, on the other hand, is used as the background color in the `TextOut` function. We will now discuss the `TextOut` function. First, we will look at the syntax of the `SetTextColor` and `SetBkColor` functions:

```
COLORREF SetTextColor(HDC hdc, COLORREF crColor);
COLORREF SetBkColor(HDC hdc, COLORREF crColor);
```

These functions appear as follows in the source code:

```
SetTextColor (hdc, RGB(0,0,180));
SetBkColor (hdc, RGB(190,180,200));
```

We will first look at the parameters of the `SetTextColor` function:

→ `hdc` is the handle to a device context object, as always. The properties are set for this device context object.

→ `crColor` is a variable of the type COLORREF. This type was discussed earlier in Chapter 2. It specifies an RGB color. This RGB color is used as a property in the device context. The `TextOut` function uses this property for the foreground color when you call the `SetTextColor` function.

The function parameters of the `SetBkColor` function are similar:

→ `hdc` is the handle to a device context object, as always. The properties are set for this device context object.

→ `crColor` is a variable of the type COLORREF. This type was discussed earlier in Chapter 2. It specifies an RGB color. This RGB color is used as a property in the device context. The `TextOut` function uses this property for the background color if you call the `SetBkColor` function.

Defining the text alignment

To define the text alignment, you must once again set the property of a device context object. You can define this property using the `SetTextAlign` function. Naturally, all the properties of a device context object that are set can be configured differently by functions. Given this, the `TextOut` function also uses these properties in an individual way. This means that if you enter TA_CENTER as a constant here, `TextOut` uses this value to position the text around the specified position. In contrast, the `DrawText` function uses this value to find the center of a specified box. The syntax of the `SetTextAlign` function is as follows:

```
UINT SetTextAlign( HDC hdc, UINT fMode);
```

This function is specified as follows in the source code:

```
SetTextAlign (hdc, TA_LEFT);
```

The function parameters are as follows:

→ `hdc` is a handle to a device context object.

→ `fMode` is a value that is specified using constants.

The Windows string functions

It may have surprised you to see that the `lstrcpy` function is used instead of `strcpy`. Windows has its own string functions. This means that you don't need any other libraries for processing strings. These functions include the following, for example: `lstrcpy`, `lstrcat`, `lstrcmp`, and `lstrlen`. An "l" is simply added at the start of the string. The syntax remains the same.

```
LPTSTR lstrcpy( LPTSTR lpString1, LPCTSTR lpString2);
```

This function is used in the following way in the source code:

```
lstrcpy (string1,"SYSTEM_FONT");
lstrcpy (string1,"SYSTEM_FIXED_FONT");
lstrcpy (string1,"ANSI_FIXED_FONT");
lstrcpy (string1,"ANSI_VAR_FONT");
lstrcpy (string1,"DEFAULT_GUI_FONT");
lstrcpy (string1,"OEM_FIXED_FONT");
```

The function parameters are as follows:

➡ lpString1 is of the type LPTSTR. This is a pointer to a char array. This function therefore requests the string, which appears at the position at which the other string is to appear.

➡ lpString2 is this other string. It is of the type LPCTSTR, which means that only the word const was added to the above type LPTSTR using this.

Displaying text

The TextOut function is used to output text. Turbo Pascal programmers, in particular, will have problems here because Turbo Pascal uses the unitgraph OutText function. Like all graphics functions, this text function is based on a handle to a device context object. It uses the values defined in the device context object by the functions SetTextColor for the foreground color, SetBkColor for the background color and the SetTextAlign function for aligning the text. The following syntax is used:

```
BOOL TextOut( HDC hdc, int nXStart, int nYStart,
              LPCTSTR lpString, int cbString);
```

This function is used in the following way:

```
TextOut (hdc, 10, 10, string1, lstrlen(string1));
TextOut (hdc, 10, 40, string1, lstrlen(string1));
TextOut (hdc, 10, 80, string1, lstrlen(string1));
TextOut (hdc, 10, 120, string1, lstrlen(string1));
TextOut (hdc, 10, 160, string1, lstrlen(string1));
TextOut (hdc, 10, 200, string1, lstrlen(string1));
```

The function parameters are explained below.

→ hdc is the handle to the device context object.

→ nXStart, nYStart are of the variable type int. They specify a position that relates to SetTextAlign. This position is specified in pixels from the top left. For example, if SetTextAlign uses the constant TA_LEFT, nXStart and nYStart define the top left corner of the text. If TA_CENTER was specified, the two values define the top center position. The text is therefore displayed around the specified point.

→ lpString is again a pointer to a char array, i.e. a string. This is the text that is displayed.

→ cbString is of the variable type int . This value specifies the number of characters to be displayed. To display the entire string, i.e. to find out the length of the string, you can use lstrlen.

You should also be familiar with the lstrlen function. You can use this to find out the length of a string:

```
int lstrlen( LPCTSTR lpString)
```

It only appears in the source code in connection with the TextOut function and includes only one function parameter:

→ lpString is the string.

→ You get the number of characters as the return value. The string's closing NULL is not counted as a character.

Control elements

4.1 General information

We use the term "control elements" to refer to buttons, edit fields or list boxes. They control communication with the user. Control elements, like all other elements on the screen, are also windows. This means that control elements are created using the `CreateWindow` function. The window class BUTTON is therefore specified for a button. This window class is defined in the same way as all the others. The Windows control elements do not have any special position and have a message processing function. When the control element receives the WM_PAINT message, it draws a button in its window. It also responds to mouse clicks. If the control element gets a mouse click on the button, it automatically sends the BN_CLICKED message. For the control elements, you normally specify a window that is above the others in the window hierarchy. This normally only affects the graphic, e.g. the positioning of the window and the graphics display within the parent window only. Windows control elements also react to this hierarchy. They determine the parent window and issue the WM_COMMAND message to this window when the button is clicked. Since the Windows control elements send a message to the parent windows, these independent windows appear to be attributes of the parent window. But they are not. The most important thing to remember here is that control elements are standard window objects. These window objects access a function for which you have no information in order to process messages. These standard Windows control elements can therefore be used very well to catch user entries.

4.2 An application

4.2.1 The source code

Our objective in this chapter is to create a control element, namely a button (see Figure 4.1). The button sends a message to the parent window and this message is processed by the sample application. The application displays all the characters of the current SYSTEM_ FONT (country-specific ANSI (see Figure 4.2)). The output from the keyboard driver is adapted to suit these characters, depending on the country setting. The keyboard driver evaluates the key's scan code. If you have opted for the English keyboard layout, the scan codes are accordingly assigned the values of the English ANSI character set. The English ANSI character set and the English keyboard layout (and keyboard driver) are defined uniquely when you install Windows. However, every ANSI character set is based on the ISO character set. One ANSI character set can also be valid for a number of countries. TrueType fonts are also ANSI character sets, but for different countries. The main difference between these and system character sets, such as the SYSTEM_FONT, for example, is the way in which the characters are defined. The system fonts are defined by pixels, just like images. The TrueType fonts are defined by vectors and other features, and must first be calculated. The system character sets are copied quickly pixel-by-pixel.

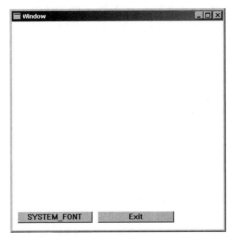

Figure 4.1 *The application after you start it*

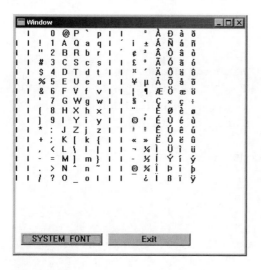

Figure 4.2 *The application after you click the SYSTEM_FONT button*

```
#include <windows.h>

LRESULT CALLBACK WndProc (HWND, UINT, WPARAM, LPARAM);

HINSTANCE hInstGlobal;

int APIENTRY WinMain(HINSTANCE hInstance,
                     HINSTANCE hPrevInstance,
                     LPSTR     lpCmdLine,
                     int       nCmdShow )
{
   hInstGlobal = hInstance;

   WNDCLASS WndClass;
   WndClass.style = 0;
   WndClass.cbClsExtra = 0;
   WndClass.cbWndExtra = 0;
   WndClass.lpfnWndProc = WndProc;
   WndClass.hInstance = hInstance;
   WndClass.hbrBackground = (HBRUSH) (COLOR_WINDOW+1);
   WndClass.hCursor = LoadCursor (NULL, IDC_ARROW);
   WndClass.hIcon = LoadIcon (NULL, IDI_APPLICATION);
   WndClass.lpszMenuName = 0;
   WndClass.lpszClassName = "WinProg";
```

```
RegisterClass(&WndClass);

HWND hWindow;
hWindow = CreateWindow("WinProg","Window",
                       WS_OVERLAPPEDWINDOW,
                       0,0,400,400,NULL,NULL,
                       hInstance, NULL);

ShowWindow (hWindow, nCmdShow);

UpdateWindow (hWindow);

MSG Message;
while (GetMessage(&Message, NULL, 0, 0))
{
   DispatchMessage(&Message)
}

return (Message.wParam);
}

LRESULT CALLBACK WndProc (HWND hWnd, UINT uiMessage,
                          WPARAM wParam,LPARAM lParam)
{
   switch(uiMessage)
   {
     case WM_CREATE:
        HWND hButton, hButtonExit;
        hButton = CreateWindow("BUTTON","SYSTEM_FONT",
                               WS_CHILD | WS_VISIBLE |
                               BS_PUSHBUTTON,
                               10,340,140,20,
                               hWnd,(HMENU) 1,

                               hInstGlobal, NULL);
        hButtonExit = CreateWindow("BUTTON","Exit",
                                   WS_CHILD |
                                   WS_VISIBLE |
                                   BS_PUSHBUTTON,
                                   160,340,140,20,
                                   hWnd,(HMENU) 2,
                                   hInstGlobal, NULL);
```

```
      return 0;
case WM_COMMAND:
   if (HIWORD(wParam) == BN_CLICKED)
   {
      if (LOWORD(wParam) == 1)
      {
         HDC hdc;
         hdc = GetDC (GetParent((HWND) lParam));
         HFONT hFont;
         hFont = (HFONT)
                 GetStockObject(SYSTEM_FONT);
         SelectObject (hdc, hFont);
         TEXTMETRIC tm;
         GetTextMetrics (hdc, &tm);
         int i;
         int ix,iy;
         ix = 0;
         iy = 0;
         char *string;
         string = new char[2];
         string[1] = 0;
         for (i=0;i<=255;i++)
         {
            string[0] = i;
            TextOut (hdc, ix, iy, string,
                     lstrlen(string));
            iy = iy + tm.tmHeight;
            if ((iy/tm.tmHeight) == 16)
            {
               iy = 0;

               ix = ix + 20;
            }
         }
         ReleaseDC (GetParent((HWND) lParam), hdc);
         delete [] string;
      }
      if (LOWORD(wParam) == 2)
      {
         SendMessage (GetParent((HWND)lParam),
                      WM_DESTROY ,0 ,0);
```

```
                }
            }
            return 0;
        case WM_DESTROY:
            PostQuitMessage(0);
            return 0;
        default:
            return DefWindowProc (hWnd, uiMessage,
                                    wParam, lParam);
    }
}
```

4.2.2   Explanation of the source code

The source code is again similar to that used in Chapter 2. Given this, we will only discuss the most important changes here.

Creating a control element

The most important change is in the window function of the `hWindow` window object. The WM_CREATE message is processed there. This message is entered in the queue when you create the window object. Other window objects are then created. In this case, these are control elements. You can use the `CreateWindow` function to create a window of the class BUTTON. It is a lower-order or child window to the main window `hWindow`. This is displayed as a parameter of `CreateWindow` by the value of `hWindow` and is determined by WS_STYLE. An ID code is appended to the window object using the value 1. When I talk about a window in this section, I actually mean the window object. Otherwise, only the area of the screen to which the window object relates is called the window. Now, let's look at the `CreateWindow` function:

```
HWND CreateWindow(LPCTSTR lpClassName,
                LPCTSTR lpWindowName,
                DWORD dwStyle,
                int x,
                int y,
                int nWidth,
                int nHeight,
                HWND hWndParent,
                HMENU hMenu,
                HANDLE hInstance,
                LPVOID lpParam
                );
```

This function is needed twice for creating control elements:

```
hButton = CreateWindow("BUTTON","SYSTEM_FONT",
                       WS_CHILD | WS_VISIBLE |
                       BS_PUSHBUTTON,
                       10,340,140,20,
                       hWnd,(HMENU) 1,
                       hInstGlobal, NULL);
hButtonExit = CreateWindow("BUTTON","Exit",
                       WS_CHILD |
                       WS_VISIBLE |
                       BS_PUSHBUTTON,
                       160,340,140,20,
                       hWnd,(HMENU)2,
                       hInstGlobal, NULL);
```

The important parameters here are as follows:

➔ lpClassName is again the name of the window class. This time, we are using the window class of the type BUTTON. The function to which this window class relates is also predefined. This creates a standard window object.

➔ lpWindowName is not used to specify the name in this case. The function of the window object uses this value to label the button in the same way as you can create a window object using the WS_POPUP attribute and the value from the lpWindowName parameter. If the WS_POPUP attribute appears instead of WS_OVERLAPPEDWINDOW, the DefWindowProc function interprets the WS_POPUP entry as meaning that a window without any extras was requested. You can then query the transferring string and use it with GDI functions.

➔ dwStyle is also changed. The WS_CHILD constant must also be specified now. The other Windows functions react to this in the graphic sense because this window is only displayed now if the parent window is also displayed. The purpose of this hierarchy was to create a structure that reflects how the window displays belong together. There are parent windows – these are not of the type WS_CHILD. The desktop window, which the system creates first, is also one of these windows.

➔ The x, y coordinates always relate to the parent window. They never relate to the screen if a WS_CHILD was set because there is no parent window.

➔ The parent window object is specified in hwndParent. This parameter must be NULL if no WS_CHILD is set.

→ Since control elements do not normally have a menu, this parameter is used to assign a number to the window object. This number can then identify the control element.

The WM_COMMAND message

The next change is the way in which the WM_COMMAND message is handled. When clicked, the window objects of the type BUTTON send a message to the parent window. This can be followed by an action, which you define under WM_COMMAND. In this case, the action involves displaying a character set – the ANSI character set of the English code page, to be precise. We use the term "code page" to refer to the various character sets that include relevant country-specific differences. Naturally, the WM_COMMAND message has a number of values in its transfer parameters:

```
WM_COMMAND
wNotifyCode = HIWORD(wParam);
wID = LOWORD(wParam);
hwndCtl = (HWND) lParam;
```

HIWORD and LOWORD are macros. Since all the parameters are of the type 32-bit integer, you can determine the upper and lower 16 bits individually. The LOWORD and HIWORD macros do this.

→ wNotifyCode is a value that is determined by the button type. A button with the style BS_PUSHBUTTON returns the value BN_CLICKED, where BN stands for *Button Notification*.
→ wID is the ID value that was transferred for CreateWindow.
→ hwndCtl is the handle to the window object, i.e. the control element that sends the message.

The first part of WM_COMMAND

```
HDC hdc;
hdc = GetDC (GetParent((HWND) lParam));
HFONT hFont;
hFont = (HFONT)
        GetStockObject(SYSTEM_FONT);
SelectObject (hdc, hFont);
```

There is nothing very new in the first part of WM_COMMAND. Only the handle to the device context object is determined here and the SYSTEM_FONT is assigned to the device context object. The only new function here is GetParent. You can use this to determine the parent window. This involves specifying the handle to the window object from which the parent window object is to be determined.

The second part of WM_COMMAND

```
TEXTMETRIC tm;
GetTextMetrics (hdc, &tm);
```

The GetTextMetrics function is used in the second part. This function returns information about the character set. The information relates to the character set, which is linked as an object to the device context object. The information is supplied in a structure with the following layout:

```
typedef struct tagTEXTMETRIC
{
    LONG tmHeight;
    LONG tmAscent;
    LONG tmDescent;
    LONG tmInternalLeading;
    LONG tmExternalLeading;
    LONG tmAveCharWidth;
    LONG tmMaxCharWidth;
    LONG tmWeight;
    LONG tmOverhang;
    LONG tmDigitizedAspectX;
    LONG tmDigitizedAspectY;
    BCHAR tmFirstChar;
    BCHAR tmLastChar;
    BCHAR tmDefaultChar;
    BCHAR tmBreakChar;
    BYTE tmItalic;
    BYTE tmUnderlined;
    BYTE tmStruckOut;
    BYTE tmPitchAndFamily;
    BYTE tmCharSet;
} TEXTMETRIC;
```

We will now look at the most important elements of the structure:

→ tmHeight is of the type LONG and is a 32-bit signed integer, just like most of the others. You must understand here that a character is made up of an ascent and a descent, which is the same as a top and bottom part. This is based on a baseline. Ascent is therefore the number of pixels above the characters' baseline, while descent is the number of pixels below. tmHeight are the two values together.

→ tmAscent is the ascent value of the characters.

→ tmDescent is the descent value of the characters.

→ tmAveCharWeight is the average width of the characters in pixels. Naturally, this value relates to the font, i.e. the character set.

→ tmMaxCharWeight is the maximum width of the characters in pixels in the font.

Only the value of the tmHeight variable is used in this source code, however. We will now look once again at the exact syntax of the GetTextMetrics function. You can use this to fill in the variables of the tm structure of the type TEXT-METRIC:

```
BOOL GetTextMetrics(HDC hdc, LPTEXTMETRIC lptm);
```

This function appears in the following way in the source code:

```
GetTextMetrics (hdc, &tm);
```

The function parameters can be explained as follows:

→ hdc is the handle to a device context object from which you want to get information about the font object that is linked to the device context object.

→ lptm is the pointer to a structure of the type TEXTMETRIC.

The third part of WM_COMMAND

```
int i;
int ix,iy;
ix = 0;
iy = 0;
char *string;
string = new char[2];
string[1] = 0;
for (i=0;i<=255;i++)
{
    string[0] = i;
    TextOut (hdc, ix, iy, string,
             lstrlen(string));
    iy = iy + tm.tmHeight;
    if ((iy/tm.tmHeight) == 16)
    {
        iy = 0;
        ix = ix + 20;
    }
}
ReleaseDC (GetParent((HWND) lParam), hdc);
delete [] string
```

The third part of the WM_COMMAND message involves displaying characters on the screen. Naturally, these characters are only displayed within the window.

To do this, a string is alternately filled with the values from 0 through 255 and displayed. The characters are displayed in 16 blocks each. The loop is responsible for this. The vertical space that a character needs is determined using `tm.tmHeight`. Otherwise, there is nothing very new here.

The fourth part of WM_COMMAND

```
if (LOWORD(wParam) == 2)
{
    SendMessage (GetParent((HWND)lParam),
                 WM_DESTROY ,0 ,0);
}
}
return 0;
```

Clicking the Exit button in the last part of the message triggers an action. A very important function, `SendMessage`, is used here. This function sends a message to the relevant application. There are two possible procedures for doing this. If you want the function to send the message to the same application from which the call is made, the window function is called immediately. If you want to send the message to a different application, however, it is simply added to the queue for this other application. The following problem arises here: The code of the application sending the message is only executed further when this message has been processed by the other application. The syntax of the `SendMessage` function is shown below:

```
LRESULT SendMessage(HWND hWnd, UINT Msg,
                    WPARAM wParam,
                    LPARAM lParam);
```

This function appears as follows in the source code:

```
SendMessage (GetParent((HWND)lParam),
             WM_DESTROY ,0 ,0);
```

Now, let's look at the function parameters:

→ `hWnd` is the handle of a window object to which the message is sent.
→ `Msg` is the value that identifies the message.
→ `wParam` is the first parameter of the message.
→ `lParam` is the second parameter of the message.

This is followed by a `return value`.

The edit field control element 5

5.1 General information

Another control element is the EDIT control element. This is an input field (or edit field) for text. You can enter text here. Like the BUTTON control element, this control element can also appear in a number of variants. We will only look at the simple variant in this chapter.

5.2 An application

5.2.1 The source code

This application is an extension of the application from Chapter 4. You must be able to enter a name in the edit field (see Figure 5.1). The name is evaluated and a character set is then selected. All these character sets are predefined (see Figures 5.2 – 5.6).

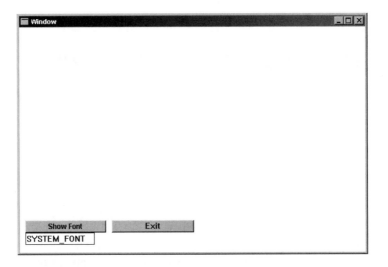

Figure 5.1 *The application after you start it*

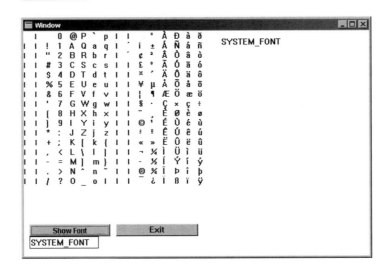

Figure 5.2 *The predefined font object SYSTEM_FONT*

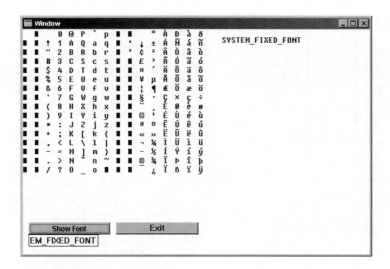

Figure 5.3 *The predefined font object SYSTEM_FIXED_FONT*

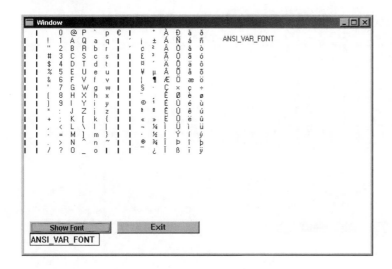

Figure 5.4 *The predefined font objects ANSI_VAR_FONT and DEFAULT_GUI_FONT with default settings*

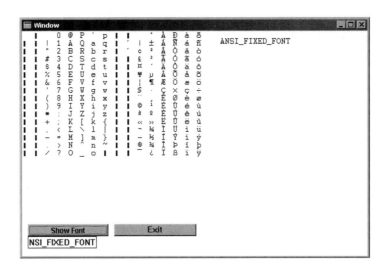

Figure 5.5   *The predefined font object ANSI_FIXED_FONT*

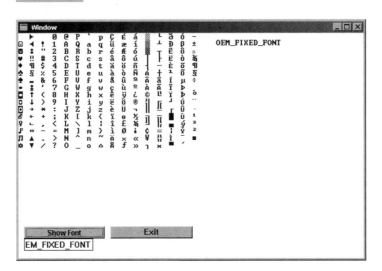

Figure 5.6   *The predefined font object OEM_FIXED_FONT*

```
#include <windows.h>

LRESULT CALLBACK WndProc (HWND, UINT, WPARAM, LPARAM);

HINSTANCE hInstGlobal;
HWND hEdit;
```

```
int APIENTRY WinMain(HINSTANCE hInstance,
                     HINSTANCE hPrevInstance,
                     LPSTR     lpCmdLine,
                     int       nCmdShow )
{
    hInstGlobal = hInstance;

    WNDCLASS WndClass;
    WndClass.style = 0;
    WndClass.cbClsExtra = 0;
    WndClass.cbWndExtra = 0;
    WndClass.lpfnWndProc = WndProc;
    WndClass.hInstance = hInstance;
    WndClass.hbrBackground = (HBRUSH) (COLOR_WINDOW+1);
    WndClass.hCursor = LoadCursor (NULL, IDC_ARROW);
    WndClass.hIcon = LoadIcon (NULL, IDI_APPLICATION);
    WndClass.lpszMenuName = 0;
    WndClass.lpszClassName = "WinProg";

    RegisterClass(&WndClass);

    HWND hWindow;
    hWindow = CreateWindow("WinProg","Window",
                           WS_OVERLAPPEDWINDOW,
                           0,0,600,400,NULL,NULL,
                           hInstance, NULL);

    ShowWindow (hWindow, nCmdShow);

    UpdateWindow (hWindow);

    MSG Message;
    while (GetMessage(&Message, NULL, 0, 0))

    {
        TranslateMessage (&Message);
        DispatchMessage(&Message);
    }

    return (Message.wParam);
}
```

```
LRESULT CALLBACK WndProc (HWND hWnd, UINT uiMessage,
                            WPARAM wParam,LPARAM lParam)
{
    switch(uiMessage)
    {
    case WM_CREATE:
        HWND hButton, hButtonExit;
        hButton = CreateWindow("BUTTON","Show Font",
                            WS_CHILD | WS_VISIBLE |
                            BS_PUSHBUTTON,
                            10,320,140,20,
                            hWnd,(HMENU) 1,
                            hInstGlobal, NULL);
        hButtonExit = CreateWindow("BUTTON","Exit",
                            WS_CHILD |
                            WS_VISIBLE |
                            BS_PUSHBUTTON,
                            160,320,140,20,
                            hWnd,(HMENU) 2,
                            hInstGlobal, NULL);
        hEdit = CreateWindow("EDIT","SYSTEM_FONT",
                            WS_CHILD | WS_VISIBLE |
                            WS_BORDER | ES_AUTOHSCROLL,
                            10,340,120,20,
                            hWnd,(HMENU) 1,
                            hInstGlobal, NULL);
        return 0;
    case WM_COMMAND:
        if (HIWORD(wParam) == BN_CLICKED)
        {

            if (LOWORD(wParam) == 1)
            {
                HDC hdc;
                hdc = GetDC (GetParent((HWND) lParam));
                HFONT hFont;
                char *string1;
                string1 = new char[255];
                SendMessage (hEdit, WM_GETTEXT, 256,
                            (LPARAM) string1);
                bool FontDa;
                FontDa = 0;
```

```
if (lstrcmp(string1,"SYSTEM_FONT") == 0)
{
   hFont = (HFONT)
           GetStockObject(SYSTEM_FONT);
   FontDa = 1;
}
if (lstrcmp(string1,"SYSTEM_FIXED_FONT")
    ==0)
{
   hFont = (HFONT)
        GetStockObject(SYSTEM_FIXED_FONT);
   FontDa = 1;
}
if (lstrcmp(string1,"OEM_FIXED_FONT") == 0)
{
   hFont = (HFONT)
           GetStockObject(OEM_FIXED_FONT);
   FontDa = 1;
}
if (lstrcmp(string1,"ANSI_VAR_FONT") == 0)
{
   hFont = (HFONT)
           GetStockObject(ANSI_VAR_FONT);
   FontDa = 1;
}
if (lstrcmp(string1,"ANSI_FIXED_FONT")==0)
{

   hFont = (HFONT)
           GetStockObject(ANSI_FIXED_FONT);
   FontDa = 1;
}
if (lstrcmp(string1,"DEFAULT_GUI_FONT")
    == 0)
{
   hFont = (HFONT)
        GetStockObject(DEFAULT_GUI_FONT);
   FontDa = 1;
}
if (FontDa == 0)
{
   hFont = (HFONT)
```

```
                    GetStockObject(SYSTEM_FONT);
        lstrcpy (string1, "SYSTEM_FONT");
    }
    SelectObject (hdc, hFont);
    RECT rect;
    SetRect (&rect, 0, 0, 480, 280);
    HBRUSH hBrush;
    hBrush = CreateSolidBrush
            (RGB(255,255,255));
    FillRect (hdc, &rect, hBrush);
    TextOut (hdc, 340, 10, string1,
            lstrlen(string1));
    delete [] string1;
    TEXTMETRIC tm;
    GetTextMetrics (hdc, &tm);
    int i;
    int ix,iy;
    ix = 0;
    iy = 0;
    char *string;
    string = new char[2];
    string[1] = 0;
    for (i=0;i<=255;i++)
    {

        string[0] = i;
        TextOut (hdc, ix, iy, string,
                lstrlen(string));
        iy = iy + tm.tmHeight;
        if ((iy/tm.tmHeight) == 16)
        {
            iy = 0;
            ix = ix + 20;
        }
    }
    ReleaseDC (GetParent((HWND) lParam), hdc);
    delete [] Editstring;
}
if (LOWORD(wParam) == 2)
{
    SendMessage (GetParent((HWND)lParam),
                WM_DESTROY ,0 ,0);
```

```
            }
        }
        return 0;
    case WM_DESTROY:
        PostQuitMessage(0);
        return 0;
    default:
        return DefWindowProc (hWnd, uiMessage,
                                wParam, lParam);
    }
}
```

5.2.2   Explanation of the source code

A few changes have been made to the source code. This is an extension of the source code from Chapter 4. You can enter text, namely the name of the constant, using the edit field. This text string is queried and compared. If the name you entered corresponds to the name of a constant, the object of this constant is linked to the device context.

The first new feature

The first notable change is the creation of the new control element. It is an edit field. We need the EDIT window class for this. We must also add WS_CHILD again. WS_CHILD now includes the additional constants WS_VISIBLE, WS_BORDER and ES_AUTOHSCROLL. WS_VISIBLE ensures that the edit field is visible immediately, while WS_BORDER displays the border. ES_AUTOHSCROLL is a style, which is only used for edit fields. It scrolls the edit field during text entry if there is not enough space available.

```
hEdit = CreateWindow("EDIT","SYSTEM_FONT",
                    WS_CHILD | WS_VISIBLE |
                    WS_BORDER | ES_AUTOHSCROLL,
                    10,340,120,20,
                    hWnd,(HMENU) 1,
                    hInstGlobal, NULL);
```

hInstGlobal is the handle to the application. This must first be passed on to a global variable.

Getting text from the edit field

You can send a message to the edit field. The text in the edit field is the window text. You can display it using the WM_GETTEXT message:

```
SendMessage (hEdit, WM_GETTEXT, 256, (LPARAM) string1);
```

```
WM_GETTEXT
wParam = (WPARAM) cchTextMax;
lParam = (LPARAM) lpszText;
```

The WM_GETTEXT message prompts you to enter a number of parameters. You must enter the maximum number of characters to be returned in `wParam`. A pointer can be passed to a `char` array, which will contain the string, in `lParam`.

Evaluating the text

As soon as you have read in the text string from the edit field, you must evaluate it. You can use a normal `if` condition for this. This condition specifies that both strings must be the same, where one comes from the edit field, while the other is a query constant. You must then decide which object you want the handle to point to. For example, you can select a font here. If you select a font, the `FontDa` variable is set to 1; if you do not select a font, the `FontDa` variable remains set to 0. You must then select the font described by SYSTEM_FONT. Finally, you must assign the handle of the font you have set to the device context object using the `SelectObject` function:

```
bool FontDa;
FontDa = 0;
if (lstrcmp(string1,"SYSTEM_FONT") == 0)
{
    hFont = (HFONT)
            GetStockObject(SYSTEM_FONT);
    FontDa = 1;
}
if (lstrcmp(string1,"SYSTEM_FIXED_FONT")
    ==0)
{
    hFont = (HFONT)
            GetStockObject(SYSTEM_FIXED_FONT);
    FontDa = 1;
}
if (lstrcmp(string1,"OEM_FIXED_FONT") == 0)
{
    hFont = (HFONT)
            GetStockObject(OEM_FIXED_FONT);
    FontDa = 1;
}
if (lstrcmp(string1,"ANSI_VAR_FONT") == 0)
{
    hFont = (HFONT)
```

```
                GetStockObject(ANSI_VAR_FONT);
      FontDa = 1;
   }
   if (lstrcmp(string1,"ANSI_FIXED_FONT")==0)
   {
      hFont = (HFONT)
                GetStockObject(ANSI_FIXED_FONT);
      FontDa = 1;
   }
   if (lstrcmp(string1,"DEFAULT_GUI_FONT")
      == 0)
   {
      hFont = (HFONT)
                GetStockObject(DEFAULT_GUI_FONT);
      FontDa = 1;
   }
   if (FontDa == 0)
   {
      hFont = (HFONT)
                GetStockObject(SYSTEM_FONT);
      lstrcpy (string1, "SYSTEM_FONT");
   }
   SelectObject (hdc, hFont);
```

There is one new function. Windows also provides an alternative for strcmp: it is called – what else would you expect – lstrcmp. This function compares two character strings. If the result indicates that the two strings are the same, the return value is 0. Otherwise, it is not 0. The function compares the characters in the sequence in which they occur and returns the difference of the first dissimilar character. If there are no differences, this value is logically 0:

```
int lstrcmp( LPCTSTR lpString1,
             LPCTSTR lpString2);
```

→ lpString1 is the first string for the comparison.
→ lpString2 is the second string for the comparison.

Getting ready to rewrite data

You must now prepare the old drawing area so that you can rewrite the data. To do this, you must create a new white Brush object. You can then use this object to color the window's display area white using the FillRect function. A label is added at the edge. This label contains the name of the constant from the GetStockObject function:

```
RECT rect;
SetRect (&rect, 0, 0, 480, 280);
HBRUSH hBrush;
hBrush = CreateSolidBrush
        (RGB(255,255,255));
FillRect (hdc, &rect, hBrush);
TextOut (hdc, 340, 10, string1,
        lstrlen(string1));
```

The data is then displayed as described in Chapter 4. There is therefore no need for any further explanation here.

System shutdown 6

6.1 General information

The word *shutdown* is used to describe the process of closing or shutting down the system. This means that the system is brought to a state, in which you can power it off. There are two ways of shutting down a system in Windows. The first is to simply shut down the system so that the user can power off the PC. The second possibility shuts down the system and restarts it immediately. You can then log the user off. If your PC supports automatic shutdown, it can even power off automatically following shutdown.

6.2 An application

6.2.1 The source code

The following application is designed to show you how to use the `ExitWindowsEx` function. You want the system to execute the following actions: it should be possible to shut down and restart, shut down and power off, and you should then be able to log off. You should be able to select these actions individually. The action is to be started using the "Shutdown" button. Yet another feature should be the option "No messages to active applications". When activated, this option prevents messages from being sent to the active applications before they are terminated. Normally, messages are sent to active applications so that they can back up data (see Figure 6.1).

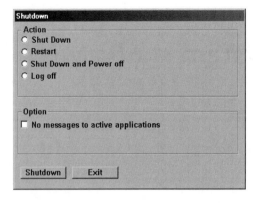

Figure 6.1 *The application after you start it*

```c
#include <windows.h>

LRESULT CALLBACK WndProc (HWND, UINT,
                            WPARAM, LPARAM);


HINSTANCE hInstGlobal;
HWND hButtonRadioButton, hButtonRadioButton2,
     hButtonRadioButton3, hButtonRadioButton4,
     hButtonCheckBox;

int APIENTRY WinMain(HINSTANCE hInstance,
                     HINSTANCE hPrevInstance,
                     LPSTR     lpCmdLine,
                     int       nCmdShow )
{
   hInstGlobal = hInstance;

   WNDCLASS WndClass;
   WndClass.style = 0;
   WndClass.cbClsExtra = 0;
   WndClass.cbWndExtra = 0;
   WndClass.lpfnWndProc = WndProc;
   WndClass.hInstance = hInstance;
   WndClass.hbrBackground = (HBRUSH)(COLOR_MENU+1);
   WndClass.hCursor = LoadCursor (NULL, IDC_ARROW);
   WndClass.hIcon = LoadIcon (NULL, IDI_APPLICATION);
   WndClass.lpszMenuName = 0;
   WndClass.lpszClassName = "WinProg";
```

```
RegisterClass(&WndClass);

int x,y;
x = GetSystemMetrics (SM_CXSCREEN);
y = GetSystemMetrics (SM_CYSCREEN);

HWND hWindow;
hWindow = CreateWindow("WinProg","Shutdown",
                    WS_OVERLAPPED,
                    (x/2)-200,(y/2),
                    150,400,300,NULL,NULL,
                    hInstance, NULL);

ShowWindow (hWindow, nCmdShow);

UpdateWindow (hWindow);

MSG Message;
while (GetMessage(&Message, NULL, 0, 0))
{
    TranslateMessage (&Message);
    DispatchMessage(&Message);
}

return (Message.wParam);
}

LRESULT CALLBACK WndProc (HWND hWnd, UINT uiMessage,
                    WPARAM wParam,LPARAM lParam)
{
    switch(uiMessage)
    {
    case WM_CREATE:

        HWND hButtonShutdown, hButtonExit,
            hButtonGroupBox, hButtonGroupBox2;
        hButtonShutdown =
            CreateWindow("BUTTON","Shutdown",
                    WS_CHILD | WS_VISIBLE |
                    BS_PUSHBUTTON,
                    10,240,80,20,
```

```
                         hWnd,(HMENU) 1,
                         hInstGlobal, NULL);
        hButtonExit =
           CreateWindow("BUTTON","Exit",
                         WS_CHILD |
                         WS_VISIBLE |
                         BS_PUSHBUTTON,
                         100,240,80,20,
                         hWnd,(HMENU) 2,
                         hInstGlobal, NULL);
        hButtonGroupBox =
           CreateWindow("BUTTON","Action",
                         WS_CHILD |
                         WS_VISIBLE |
                         BS_GROUPBOX,
                         5,5,380,120,
                         hWnd,(HMENU) 3,
                         hInstGlobal, NULL);
        hButtonRadioButton =
           CreateWindow("BUTTON","Shut down",
                         WS_CHILD |
                         WS_VISIBLE |
                         BS_RADIOBUTTON,
                         10,20,280,20,
                         hWnd,(HMENU) 4,
                         hInstGlobal, NULL);
        hButtonRadioButton2 =
           CreateWindow("BUTTON","Restart",
                         WS_CHILD |
                         WS_VISIBLE |
                         BS_RADIOBUTTON,
                         10,40,280,20,
                         hWnd,(HMENU) 5,
                         hInstGlobal, NULL);
        hButtonRadioButton3 =
           CreateWindow("BUTTON",
                         "Shut down and power off",
                         WS_CHILD |
                         WS_VISIBLE |
                         BS_RADIOBUTTON,
                         10,60,280,20,
                         hWnd,(HMENU) 6,
```

```
                              hInstGlobal, NULL);
      hButtonRadioButton4 =
         CreateWindow("BUTTON","Log off",
                        WS_CHILD |
                        WS_VISIBLE |
                        BS_RADIOBUTTON,
                        10,80,280,20,
                        hWnd,(HMENU) 7,
                        hInstGlobal, NULL);
      hButtonGroupBox2 =
         CreateWindow("BUTTON","Option",
                        WS_CHILD |
                        WS_VISIBLE |
                        BS_GROUPBOX,
                        5,140,380,80,
                        hWnd,(HMENU) 8,
                        hInstGlobal, NULL);
      hButtonCheckBox =
         CreateWindow("BUTTON",
             "No messages to active applications",
                        WS_CHILD |
                        WS_VISIBLE |
                        BS_CHECKBOX,
                        10,160,340,20,
                        hWnd,(HMENU) 9,
                        hInstGlobal, NULL);
      return 0;


   case WM_COMMAND:
      if (HIWORD(wParam) == BN_CLICKED)
      {
         if (LOWORD(wParam) == 1)
         {
          int Parameter;
          Parameter = 0;
          if (SendMessage (hButtonRadioButton,
                           BM_GETCHECK, 0, 0)
                           == BST_CHECKED)
            {
             Parameter = EWX_SHUTDOWN;
            }
          if (SendMessage (hButtonRadioButton2,
```

```
                              BM_GETCHECK, 0, 0)
                              == BST_CHECKED)
  {
   Parameter = EWX_REBOOT;
  }
 if (SendMessage (hButtonRadioButton3,
                  BM_GETCHECK, 0, 0) ==
                  BST_CHECKED)
  {
   Parameter = EWX_POWEROFF;
  }
 if (SendMessage (hButtonRadioButton4,
                  BM_GETCHECK, 0, 0) ==
                  BST_CHECKED)
  {
   Parameter = EWX_LOGOFF;
  }
 if (SendMessage (hButtonCheckBox,
                  BM_GETCHECK, 0, 0)
                  == BST_CHECKED)
  {
   Parameter = Parameter | EWX_FORCE;
  }
 ExitWindowsEx (Parameter, 0);

}
if (LOWORD(wParam) == 2)
{
   SendMessage (GetParent((HWND)lParam),
               WM_DESTROY ,0 ,0);
}
if (LOWORD(wParam) == 4)
{
 if (!(SendMessage ((HWND)lParam,
                    BM_GETCHECK, 0, 0)
                    == BST_CHECKED))
  {
   SendMessage ((HWND)lParam,
               BM_SETCHECK, BST_CHECKED, 0);
   SendMessage (hButtonRadioButton2,
               BM_SETCHECK, BST_UNCHECKED, 0);
   SendMessage (hButtonRadioButton3,
```

```
                      BM_SETCHECK, BST_UNCHECKED, 0);
  SendMessage (hButtonRadioButton4,
                      BM_SETCHECK, BST_UNCHECKED, 0);
 }


}
if (LOWORD(wParam) == 6)
{
 if (!(SendMessage ((HWND)lParam,
                      BM_GETCHECK, 0, 0)
                      == BST_CHECKED))
 {
  SendMessage ((HWND)lParam,
                      BM_SETCHECK, BST_CHECKED, 0);
  SendMessage (hButtonRadioButton,
                      BM_SETCHECK, BST_UNCHECKED, 0);
  SendMessage (hButtonRadioButton2,
                      BM_SETCHECK, BST_UNCHECKED, 0);
  SendMessage (hButtonRadioButton4,
                      BM_SETCHECK, BST_UNCHECKED, 0);
 }


}
if (LOWORD(wParam) == 7)
{
 if (!(SendMessage ((HWND)lParam,
                      BM_GETCHECK, 0, 0)
                      == BST_CHECKED))
 {
  SendMessage ((HWND)lParam,
                      BM_SETCHECK, BST_CHECKED, 0);
  SendMessage (hButtonRadioButton,
                      BM_SETCHECK, BST_UNCHECKED, 0);
  SendMessage (hButtonRadioButton3,
                      BM_SETCHECK, BST_UNCHECKED, 0);
  SendMessage (hButtonRadioButton2,
                      BM_SETCHECK, BST_UNCHECKED, 0);
 }
}
if (LOWORD(wParam) == 5)
{
 if (!(SendMessage ((HWND)lParam,
```

```
                  BM_GETCHECK, 0, 0)
                  == BST_CHECKED))
          {
           SendMessage ((HWND)lParam,
                       BM_SETCHECK, BST_CHECKED, 0);
            SendMessage (hButtonRadioButton,
                       BM_SETCHECK, BST_UNCHECKED, 0);
            SendMessage (hButtonRadioButton3,
                       BM_SETCHECK, BST_UNCHECKED, 0);
            SendMessage (hButtonRadioButton4,
                       BM_SETCHECK, BST_UNCHECKED, 0);
           }
          }
          if (LOWORD(wParam) == 9)
          {
           if (SendMessage ((HWND)lParam,
                       BM_GETCHECK, 0, 0)
                       == BST_CHECKED)

           {
            SendMessage ((HWND)lParam,
                       BM_SETCHECK, BST_UNCHECKED, 0);
           }
           else
           {
            SendMessage ((HWND)lParam,
                       BM_SETCHECK, BST_CHECKED, 0);
           }
          }
         }
        return 0;
      case WM_DESTROY:
        PostQuitMessage(0);
        return 0;
      default:
        return DefWindowProc (hWnd, uiMessage,
                             wParam, lParam);
      }
    }
```

6.2.2 Explanation of the source code

The first part of the application

We create a window in the usual way in the first part of the source code. However, this window is not created in the top left corner as usual, but is positioned in the center of the screen. Details of the screen size are needed for this. You can get these details using `GetSystemMetrics`. From these, we can work out the position that must be specified for the window to ensure that it appears in the center of the screen. We then assign the WS_OVERLAPPED property to the window. This is a window that can be overlapped by other windows and also has a title bar and a border.

Changes in the window procedure

The first thing we notice is that many control elements of the type BUTTON are created. Three new kinds of BUTTON control elements are used, namely the styles BS_RADIOBUTTON, BS_CHECKBOX, and BS_GROUPBOX. The first two are selectable buttons. The selectable buttons are generally grouped together to form group boxes , i.e. groups. Only one of the radio buttons can be enabled at any one time, while several of the check boxes can be activated at the same time. A button of the type BS_GROUPBOX is simply a frame containing a heading for these buttons.

Other changes are made in the WM_COMMAND message. For example, it must be possible to toggle the individual radio buttons on and off. To this end, the other radio buttons must all be deselected when one is selected. You must select the radio button manually. The same applies for the check boxes.

The actual main section involves querying the Shutdown button. The `ExitWindowsEx` function is used for this. The function parameters are first combined so that the function only has to be called once. We now want to look at this function in detail.

```
BOOL ExitWindowsEx( UINT uFlags,
                    DWORD dwReserved);
```

It appears in the following way in the source code:

```
ExitWindowsEx (Parameter, 0);
```

The function thus performs various actions in order to shut down the computer, or at least all the active applications, and reinitialize the operating system.

→ uFlags indicates the actions, which the ExitWindowsEx function performs. This involves five different parameters. The first four parameters cannot be combined together, but the fifth can be combined with the other four.
EWX_LOGOFF logs the user off.
EWX_POWEROFF shuts down the computer and powers it off if the corresponding hardware support is available.
EWX_REBOOT restarts the computer.
EWX_SHUTDOWN shuts down the computer.
EWX_FORCE means that no messages are sent to active applications. As a result, the active applications cannot either back up their data or influence the system deinitialization process.

→ dwReserved is ignored.

Bitmaps

7.1 General information

There are two kinds of bitmaps, namely DDBs (*device-dependent bitmaps*) and DIBs *(device-independent bitmaps)*. A bitmap is an array of data containing information about the color of pixels in an image. DDBs contain only the color information for the pixels. DIBs contain the color information as well as information about how this color data is to be interpreted. This information includes data relating to the width and height of the image, for example, and details of the color depth.

The fact that lines in a bitmap can only end with linear byte specifications is very important here because otherwise errors occur in the display.

7.1.1 DDB

DDBs contain only the simple pixel data. They are bitmaps that are created when the application is running. The reason for this is that they are only intended for use on this output device. Given that these bitmaps do not contain any information about the color depth, they cannot be mapped to a screen with a different color depth, for example. Since the function does not know how the image is to be mapped in the video memory, it simply copies the data. This results in a totally confused image.

DDBs are handled in the same way as GDI objects. Here, we have a bitmap object, which can also be assigned to a device context object. This device context must be the memory, however. This means that it cannot be a device context of the screen because the function is not running there.

7.1.2 DIB

DIBs contain the pixel data and other information about the pixels. DIBs can therefore be mapped on any screen. If a DIB has a higher color depth than the output device, the pixels are adapted to suit the output device using the information about the pixels.

7.1.3   Color depth

The color depth is a value that specifies how many colors can be displayed. You can change this setting in the control panel for the monitor and the graphics card. You set the color depth by specifying the number of bits that are to be available for a pixel. Practically all monitors – except very old ones – can display RGB colors. But graphics cards sometimes have problems with this because they do not have enough memory. The number of displayable colors is generally calculated on the basis of 2^x bits. For example, if you have 2^8 bits, this works out to be 256 different color values. For this number, however, the RGB values are taken from a color table in which the value of the pixels represents only one index. 2^{24} bits give you 16.7 million different color values. This value corresponds to True-Color. There is no color table here, but only 24 bits per pixel, where 8 bits specify each of the values for blue, red and green. You must first instruct the graphics card as to how to interpret the pixel data. You can do this in the control panel. The graphics card then converts the digital signals into analog signals, which the monitor can display. If you are using 256 color values, you must first provide the graphics card with a color table. You cannot set color depths other than 4, 8, 16 and 32 because the Windows GDI functions must be able to handle these values. The GDI functions adapt graphics with more colors to a lower color depth. Essentially, all color values in GDI functions are specified using 32-bit values, where the first 8 bits are not used. This is followed by 8 bits for each of the RGB values. The GDI functions adapt these RGB values according to the color depth of the output device. The procedure for interpreting the number of bits per pixel is defined in the same way for most graphics cards in order to send an analog color value to the monitor. The GDI functions only react to the standards.

7.2 The DDB application

7.2.1   The source code

The next application creates a DDB. DDBs are handled in the same way as GDI objects. The first step is to create a memory device context object . You can do this using the `CreateCompatibleDC` function. You then create the bitmap object. This contains the pixel data of the DDB and is assigned to the memory device context object. The next step is to assign the data from the memory device context object to the screen device context object using the `BitBlt` function. You must set the color depth to 8 bits so that the program can work. You can use the control panel to do this. Double-click the Display icon and then click the Settings tab and change the color value to 25. See Figures 7.1 – 7.3.

Figure 7.1 *The application after you start it*

Figure 7.2 *The application after you left-click ...*

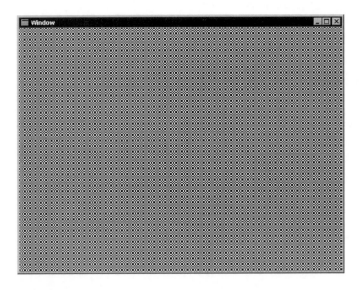

Figure 7.3 *... and after you right-click*

```c
#include <windows.h>

LRESULT CALLBACK WndProc (HWND, UINT, WPARAM, LPARAM);

int APIENTRY WinMain(HINSTANCE hInstance,
                     HINSTANCE hPrevInstance,
                     LPSTR     lpCmdLine,
                     int       nCmdShow )
{
   WNDCLASS WndClass;
   WndClass.style = 0;
   WndClass.cbClsExtra = 0;
   WndClass.cbWndExtra = 0;
   WndClass.lpfnWndProc = WndProc;
   WndClass.hInstance = hInstance;
   WndClass.hbrBackground = (HBRUSH) (COLOR_WINDOW+1);
   WndClass.hCursor = LoadCursor (NULL, IDC_ARROW);
   WndClass.hIcon = LoadIcon (NULL, IDI_APPLICATION);
   WndClass.lpszMenuName = 0;
   WndClass.lpszClassName = "WinProg";

   RegisterClass(&WndClass);

   HWND hWindow;
```

```
    hWindow = CreateWindow("WinProg","Window",
                           WS_OVERLAPPEDWINDOW,
                           0,0,600,460,NULL,NULL,
                           hInstance, NULL);


    ShowWindow (hWindow, nCmdShow);


    UpdateWindow (hWindow);


    MSG Message;
    while (GetMessage(&Message, NULL, 0, 0))
    {
        DispatchMessage(&Message);
    }



    return (Message.wParam);
}

LRESULT CALLBACK WndProc (HWND hWnd, UINT uiMessage,
                          WPARAM wParam,LPARAM lParam)
{
    static BYTE Pixel[6][5] = {0  ,255,0  ,255,0  ,0,
                               255,0  ,255,0  ,255,0,
                               0  ,255,0  ,255,0  ,0,
                               255,0  ,255,0  ,255,0,
                               0  ,255,0  ,255,0  ,0};
    static HBITMAP hBitmap;
    static HDC hdcmem;

    switch(uiMessage)
    {
        case WM_LBUTTONDOWN:
            HDC hdc;
            hdc = GetDC (hWnd);

            hdcmem = CreateCompatibleDC (hdc);
            hBitmap = CreateBitmap (6,5,1,8,Pixel);
            SelectObject (hdcmem, hBitmap);

            RECT rect;
            GetClientRect (hWnd, &rect);
            int x,y;
```

```
        for (y=0;y<rect.bottom;y=y+5)
        {
         for (x=0;x<rect.right;x=x+5)
         {
          BitBlt (hdc,x,y,5,5,hdcmem,0,0,SRCCOPY);
         }
        }

        DeleteObject (hBitmap);
        DeleteDC (hdcmem);

        ReleaseDC (hWnd, hdc);
        return 0;
    case WM_RBUTTONDOWN:
        hdc = GetDC (hWnd);

        hdcmem = CreateCompatibleDC (hdc);
        hBitmap = CreateBitmap (5,5,1,8,Pixel);
        SelectObject (hdcmem, hBitmap);

        GetClientRect (hWnd, &rect);
        for (y=0;y<rect.bottom;y=y+10)
        {
         for (x=0;x<rect.right;x=x+10)
         {
          StretchBlt (hdc,x,y,10,10,
                          hdcmem,0,0,5,5,SRCCOPY);
         }
        }

        DeleteObject (hBitmap);
        DeleteDC (hdcmem);
        ReleaseDC (hWnd, hdc);
        return 0;
    case WM_DESTROY:
        PostQuitMessage(0);
        return 0;
    default:
        return DefWindowProc (hWnd, uiMessage,
                              wParam, lParam);
    }
}
```

7.2.2 Explanation of the source code

Changes have only been made to the WndProc function.

New variables

A number of new variables are declared:

```
static BYTE Pixel[6][5] = {0   ,255,0   ,255,0   ,0,
                           255,0   ,255,0   ,255,0,
                           0   ,255,0   ,255,0   ,0,
                           255,0   ,255,0   ,255,0,
                           0   ,255,0   ,255,0   ,0};
static HBITMAP hBitmap;
static HDC hdcmem;
```

→ The pixel array contains the data relating to the pixels. The image actually has 5x5 pixels. A pixel line must end with a linear number of pixels. The bitmap therefore has 6x5 pixels. This is the actual pixel data.

→ hBitmap is the handle to the bitmap object. We will create this later.

→ hdcmem is a standard handle to a device context object. In this case, the device context is not part of the screen, but part of the memory that simulates a graphics device context.

The WM_LBUTTONDOWN message

The WM_LBUTTONDOWN message displays a window when you click in the message with the left mouse button. The program's main function is then executed.

```
HDC hdc;
hdc = GetDC (hWnd);

hdcmem = CreateCompatibleDC (hdc);
hBitmap = CreateBitmap (6,5,1,8,Pixel);
SelectObject (hdcmem, hBitmap);

RECT rect;
GetClientRect (hWnd, &rect);
int x,y;
for (y=0;y<rect.bottom;y=y+5)
{
   for (x=0;x<rect.right;x=x+5)
   {
      BitBlt (hdc,x,y,5,5,hdcmem,0,0,SRCCOPY);
   }
}
```

```
}

DeleteDC (hdcmem);
ReleaseDC (hWnd, hdc);
return 0;
```

CreateCompatibleDC

First, we must determine the device context handle of the main window. We then create a memory device context object. This memory device context must be compatible with the device context of the window. All this is possible using the `CreateCompatibleDC` function:

```
HDC CreateCompatibleDC( HDC hdc);
```

This command is used twice in the same way in the source code:

```
hdcmem = CreateCompatibleDC (hdc);
```

➜ hdc is the handle to the device context object, which we want to use to create the memory device context object.

CreateBitmap

We then create a Bitmap object using the `CreateBitmap` function. The Bitmap object then contains the data for the bitmap, i.e. the pixels. Since a DDB is created in this way, this object does not contain any data relating to how the pixels were stored, i.e. which color depth was used. We must enter these values.

```
HBITMAP CreateBitmap( int nWidth, int nHeight,
                      UINT cPlanes, UINT cBitsPerPixel,
                      CONST VOID *lpvBits);
```

This function appears twice in the source code:

```
hBitmap = CreateBitmap (6,5,1,8,Pixel);
```

➜ nWidth and nHeight specify the width and height of the bitmap (DDB).
➜ cPlanes is the number of color levels or planes. This value is not relevant and is therefore set to 1.
➜ cBitsPerPixel is a value that specifies the number of bits per pixel.
➜ lpvBits is a pointer to the memory area in which the pixels are stored.

GetClientRect

We then assign the bitmap object to the device context object and declare a structure of the type RECT. This structure is needed for the `GetClientRect` function. We use this function to retrieve the data about the box in the device context object of the window. This data is specified in pixels and relates to the top left corner of the device context:

```
BOOL GetClientRect ( HWND hWnd, LPRECT lpRect);
```

This function is also used twice in the source code:

```
GetClientRect (hWnd, &rect);
```

→ hWnd is the handle to the window object from which we want to determine the dimensions of the device context object.

→ lpRect is a pointer to a structure of the type RECT in which the dimensions of the device context object are stored.

BitBlt

The next step is to copy data relating to the memory device context object to the device context object of the screen. We use the BitBlt function for this. Since we want this bitmap to fill the entire area of the device context object, we must copy it a number of times at regular intervals into the device context object of the screen:

```
BOOL BitBlt ( HDC hdcDest, int nXDest, int nYDest,
              int nWidth, int nHeight, HDC hdcSrc,
              int nXSrc, int nYSrc, DWORD dwRop);
```

This function appears twice in the source code:

```
BitBlt (hdc,x,y,5,5,hdcmem,0,0,SRCCOPY);
```

→ hdcDest is the handle to the device context object into which we want to copy the image data.

→ nXDest and nYDest specify the position to which the image data is to be copied.

→ nWidth and nHeight are the width and height of the image data that we want to copy. They relate to both the source object and the destination object.

→ hdcSrc is the handle to the device context object from which the data is copied.

→ nXSrc and nYSrc specify the position in the source object from which the image data is to be copied.

→ dwRop is a value containing constants. One of these is declared under the name SRCCPY. This constant states that the source box is copied to the destination box using image data.

DeleteDC

We will now delete the memory device context object. We use the `DeleteDC` function for this. We will then release the handle to the device context object of the screen.

```
BOOL DeleteDC( HDC hdc);
```

The function looks like this in the source code:

```
DeleteDC (hdcmem);
```

→ hdc is the handle to the device context object, which we want to delete.

The **WM_RBUTTONDOWN** message

When this message appears, the same thing happens as for WM_LBUTTONDOWN. There is a difference, however: the pixel data is copied using the `StretchBlt` function. As a result, the pixel data appears magnified:

```
BOOL StretchBlt(HDC hdcDest, int nXOriginDest,
                int nYOriginDest, int nWidthDest,
                int nHeightDest, HDC hdcSrc,
                int nXOriginSrc, int nYOriginSrc,
                int nWidthSrc, int nHeightSrc,
                DWORD dwRop);
```

This function appears in the following way in the source code:

```
StretchBlt (hdc,x,y,10,10,
             hdcmem,0,0,5,5,SRCCOPY);
```

→ hdcDest is the handle to the device context object to which you want to copy the image data.

→ nXOriginDest and nYOriginDest specify the position to which you want to copy the image data.

→ nWidthDest and nHeightDest are the width and height of the image data which you want to copy. These relate to the destination object. They also indicate the degree of magnification of the image data.

→ hdcSrc is the handle to the device context object from which the data is copied.

→ nXOriginSrc and nYOriginSrc specify the position in the source object from which the image data is to be copied.

→ nWidthSrc and nHeightSrc are the width and height of the image data, which you want to copy. These relate to the source object.

→ dwRop is a value containing constants. One of these is declared under the name SRCCPY. This constant states that the source box is copied to the destination box using image data.

7.3 The DIB application

7.3.1   The source code

This application loads a bitmap file, i.e. a BMP file, from the hard disk into the memory. It is therefore a DIB file as also created by Paintbrush. Since a DIB is made up of several structures, a certain amount of memory from the main memory is allocated to each of these structures. The image data is adapted to suit the output device and is then displayed on the screen. The memory is then released again. See Figures 7.4 – 7.5.

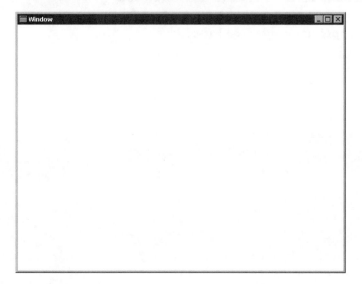

Figure 7.4 *The application after you start it*

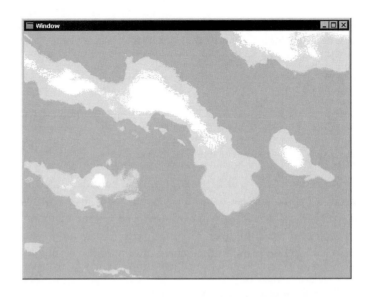

Figure 7.5 *The application after you left-click*

```c
#include <windows.h>

LRESULT CALLBACK WndProc (HWND, UINT, WPARAM, LPARAM);

int APIENTRY WinMain(HINSTANCE hInstance,
                     HINSTANCE hPrevInstance,
                     LPSTR     lpCmdLine,
                     int       nCmdShow )
{
    WNDCLASS WndClass;
    WndClass.style = 0;
    WndClass.cbClsExtra = 0;
    WndClass.cbWndExtra = 0;
    WndClass.lpfnWndProc = WndProc;
    WndClass.hInstance = hInstance;
    WndClass.hbrBackground = (HBRUSH) (COLOR_WINDOW+1);
    WndClass.hCursor = LoadCursor (NULL, IDC_ARROW);
    WndClass.hIcon = LoadIcon (NULL, IDI_APPLICATION);
    WndClass.lpszMenuName = 0;
    WndClass.lpszClassName = "WinProg";

    RegisterClass(&WndClass);
```

```
HWND hWindow;
hWindow = CreateWindow("WinProg","Window",
                       WS_OVERLAPPEDWINDOW,
                       0,0,600,460,NULL,NULL,
                       hInstance, NULL);

ShowWindow (hWindow, nCmdShow);

UpdateWindow (hWindow);

MSG Message;
while (GetMessage(&Message, NULL, 0, 0))
{
    DispatchMessage(&Message);
}


return (Message.wParam);
}

LRESULT CALLBACK WndProc (HWND hWnd, UINT uiMessage,
                          WPARAM wParam,LPARAM lParam)
{
    static BITMAPFILEHEADER *pbmfh;
    static BITMAPINFO *pbmi;
    static BYTE *pBits;
    static int cxDib, cyDib;

    switch(uiMessage)
    {
        case WM_LBUTTONDOWN:
            DWORD dwFileSize, dwHighSize, dwBytesRead;
            HANDLE hFile;
            hFile = CreateFile ("C:\\test.bmp", GENERIC_READ,
                                FILE_SHARE_READ, NULL,
                                OPEN_EXISTING,
                                FILE_FLAG_SEQUENTIAL_SCAN,
                                NULL);
            dwFileSize = GetFileSize (hFile, &dwHighSize);
            pbmfh = (BITMAPFILEHEADER *) malloc (dwFileSize);
            ReadFile (hFile, pbmfh, dwFileSize,
                      &dwBytesRead, NULL);
```

```
pbmi = (BITMAPINFO *) (pbmfh + 1);
pBits = (BYTE *) pbmfh + pbmfh->bfOffBits;
cxDib = pbmi->bmiHeader.biWidth;
cyDib = abs(pbmi->bmiHeader.biHeight);
HDC hdc;
hdc = GetDC (hWnd);

SetDIBitsToDevice (hdc,
                   0,
                   0,
                   cxDib,
                   cyDib,

                   0,
                   0,
                   0,
                   cyDib,
                   pBits,
                   pbmi,
                   DIB_RGB_COLORS);

    ReleaseDC (hWnd, hdc);
    free (pbmfh);
    return 0;
case WM_DESTROY:
    PostQuitMessage(0);
    return 0;
default:
    return DefWindowProc (hWnd, uiMessage,
                          wParam, lParam);
    }
}
```

7.3.2   Explanation of the source code

The first changes in this source code are in the WM_LBUTTONDOWN message:

New variables
```
static BITMAPFILEHEADER *pbmfh;
static BITMAPINFO *pbmi;
static BYTE *pBits;
static int cxDib, cyDib;
```

Two new pointers to structures are added. The structures are of the type BITMAPFILEHEADER and BITMAPINFO. A pointer to variables of the type Byte is also created. Another two correct variables are then declared.

The BITMAPFILEHEADER structure is used to store information about the type, size and layout of a DIB:

```
typedef struct tagBITMAPFILEHEADER
{
    WORD      bfType;
    DWORD     bfSize;
    WORD      bfReserved1;
    WORD      bfReserved2;
    DWORD     bfOffBits;
} BITMAPFILEHEADER;
```

→ bfType specifies the file type. We talk about a file type because DIBs are usually loaded from files. The file type must be "BM".

→ bfSize is the size of the bitmap file in bytes.

→ bfReserved1 and bfReserved2 should both be NULL.

→ bfOffBits is the number of bytes, counting from the start of the DIB file to the actual pixel data.

The BITMAPINFO structure contains information about the size and color depth of the bitmap. Naturally, the bitmap is a DIB:

```
typedef struct tagBITMAPINFO
{
    BITMAPINFOHEADER bmiHeader;
    RGBQUAD          bmiColors[1];
} BITMAPINFO;
```

→ The two variables of the BITMAPINFO structure are themselves structures.

Reading in the file

The next thing we have to do is to read in the DIB file. We will not discuss the functions used for working with files in any great detail now. The fact remains that the file is read into a previously reserved memory area. The start of this memory area then forms the start of the pbmfh structure:

```
DWORD dwFileSize, dwHighSize, dwBytesRead;
HANDLE hFile;
hFile = CreateFile ("C:\\test.bmp", GENERIC_READ,
                    FILE_SHARE_READ, NULL,
```

```
                  OPEN_EXISTING,
                  FILE_FLAG_SEQUENTIAL_SCAN,
                  NULL);
dwFileSize = GetFileSize (hFile, &dwHighSize);
pbmfh = (BITMAPFILEHEADER *) malloc (dwFileSize);
ReadFile (hFile, pbmfh, dwFileSize,
          &dwBytesRead, NULL);
```

Defining the structures

The pointer from pbmfh is set to the start of the file that was read in. These structures would already be assigned in this way. The next structure follows directly after this and is of the type BITMAPINFO. This structure can also be different, depending on which Windows version you are using. (It can even be a completely different structure, as in the original OS/2 version, for example.) We will now define the position of the pixel data. We will then store specific data from these structures in variables, including the height and width of the image:

```
pbmi = (BITMAPINFO *) (pbmfh + 1);
pBits = (BYTE *) pbmfh + pbmfh->bfOffBits;
cxDib = pbmi->bmiHeader.biWidth;
cyDib = abs(pbmi->bmiHeader.biHeight);
```

SetDIBitsToDevice

We will now determine a handle to the device context object, in which the bitmap is to be displayed. We will then use the SetDIBitToDevice function to adapt the pixels to the color depth of the output device. The pixels are then mapped to the output device:

```
int SetDIBitsToDevice( HDC hdc, int XDest, int YDest,
                       DWORD dwWidth, DWORD dwHeight,
                       int XSrc, int YSrc,
                       UINT uStartScan, UINT cScanLines,
                       CONST VOID *lpvBits,
                       CONST BITMAPINFO *lpbmi,
                       UINT fuColorUse);
```

The function looks like this in the source code:

```
SetDIBitsToDevice (hdc,
                   0,
                   0,
                   cxDib,
                   cyDib,
```

```
0,
0,
0,
cyDib,
pBits,
pbmi,
DIB_RGB_COLORS);
```

→ hdc is the handle to the device context object.

→ Xdest and Ydest specify the relative position in the destination device in pixels.

→ dwWidth and dwHeight are the width and height of the bitmap.

→ XSrc and YSrc specify the position in the source structure.

→ uStartScan is the first ScanLine in the DIB.

→ cScanLine is the number of scan lines in the DIB.

→ lpvBits is the pointer to the pixel data.

→ lpbmi is the pointer to the BITMAPINFO structure.

→ fuColorUse is a DIB_RGB_COLORS constant. It states that standard RGB values must be used here.

Menus 8

8.1 General information

This chapter deals with the creation of menus for windows. A menu is a list of items, which show the actions of an application. The menu bar is almost always located beneath the title bar (see Figure 8.1). Clicking on the menu bar triggers certain actions for the program.

Figure 8.1   *The editor's menu bar beneath the title bar*

A menu is not a window object, but a menu object, which the window object can access. A menu object belongs to a window object. A window object is characterized by the fact that it has a message processing function, which the application calls in order to display and manage the window. A menu object is therefore simply a data structure that does not draw itself, but is used by the window object. In other words, the window object's function uses the information about the menu object to draw a menu in the window.

A menu bar is created by a series of objects. You therefore create menu objects and assign entries to them. For example, a menu item can initiate a function or refer to a submenu. This establishes a hierarchy. A menu is created and provided with menu items. An ID number is assigned to all the menu items that are to initiate an action. New menu objects are then created. These new menu objects are submenu objects, which in turn contain menu items and are not actually any different from the other menu objects. The menu items can also initiate an action. You assign these submenu objects as a menu item to the previously created menu object. The first object in a menu is always a normal menu object. All the other menu objects are submenu objects. Linking with menu items produces a hierarchy. The highest item in the hierarchy (i.e. the menu object) is assigned to the window.

The highest menu object is displayed in the menu bar. The window's menu bar is always visible in the window, but the submenus are not. Entries in menu bars should not initiate any functions, but should refer to submenus. Of course, the menu bar can also contain menu items that do actually initiate functions.

Only windows of the type WS_OVERLAPPED and WS_POPUP can contain menus.

The actions that can initiate menu items are controlled by the window's message processing function. When you select a menu item, a message is entered in the queue for the window to which the menu belongs. This message is assigned the ID number of the menu item.

Menu items can be initiated using standard keys. This service is provided automatically.

A menu object must not be deleted from the application before it is terminated. If the menu object is linked to the window object, it is deleted when you delete the window object. However, if the menu object is not linked to a window object, you must delete it at the end of the application.

8.2 An application

8.2.1 The source code

This program allows you to create and display a window. You can then create a hierarchy of menu objects. The highest menu object is assigned to the window object. This means that the program has a menu. Table 8.1 below shows the structure of the menu. See also Figures 8.2 and 8.3.

Menu item Level 1	Menu item Level 2	Menu item Level 3	Action or reference
Draw Box			
File			
	Exit		
Information			
	Author		
	Graphic		
		Color depth	
		Resolution	
	Hard disk		
		Windows directory	

Menu item Level 1	Menu item Level 2	Menu item Level 3	Action or reference
		Current directory	

Table 8.1 *The application's menu*

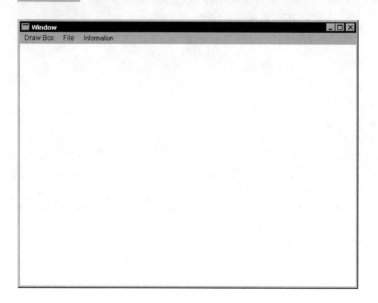

Figure 8.2 *The application after you start it*

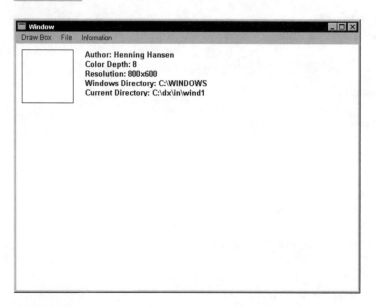

Figure 8.3 *The application after executing most of the menu items*

```
#include <windows.h>

LRESULT CALLBACK WndProc (HWND, UINT, WPARAM, LPARAM);

int APIENTRY WinMain(HINSTANCE hInstance,
                     HINSTANCE hPrevInstance,
                     LPSTR     lpCmdLine,
                     int       nCmdShow )
{

    WNDCLASS WndClass;
    WndClass.style = 0;
    WndClass.cbClsExtra = 0;
    WndClass.cbWndExtra = 0;
    WndClass.lpfnWndProc = WndProc;
    WndClass.hInstance = hInstance;
    WndClass.hbrBackground = (HBRUSH) (COLOR_WINDOW+1);
    WndClass.hCursor = LoadCursor (NULL, IDC_ARROW);
    WndClass.hIcon = LoadIcon (NULL, IDI_APPLICATION);
    WndClass.lpszMenuName = 0;
    WndClass.lpszClassName = "Prog8";

    RegisterClass(&WndClass);

    HWND hWindow;
    hWindow = CreateWindow("Prog8","Window",
                           WS_OVERLAPPEDWINDOW,
                           0,0,600,460,NULL,NULL,
                           hInstance, NULL);

    ShowWindow (hWindow, nCmdShow);

    UpdateWindow (hWindow);

    MSG Message;
    while (GetMessage(&Message, NULL, 0, 0))
    {
        DispatchMessage(&Message);
    }

    return (Message.wParam);
}
```

```
LRESULT CALLBACK WndProc (HWND hWnd, UINT uiMessage,

                                WPARAM wParam,LPARAM lParam)
{
    switch(uiMessage)
    {
        case WM_CREATE:
            HMENU hMenu;
            hMenu = CreateMenu ();
            MENUITEMINFO mii;
            mii.cbSize = sizeof(MENUITEMINFO);
            mii.fMask = MIIM_TYPE | MIIM_ID;
            mii.fType = MFT_STRING;

            char *string;
            string = new char[40];
            lstrcpy (string,"Draw Box");
            mii.dwTypeData = string;
            mii.cch = lstrlen (string);
            mii.fState = MFS_ENABLED;
            mii.wID = 1;
            InsertMenuItem (hMenu, 0, FALSE,  &mii);

                HMENU hMenu2;
                hMenu2 = CreatePopupMenu ();
                lstrcpy (string, "Exit");
                mii.wID = 2;
                InsertMenuItem (hMenu2, 0, FALSE,  &mii);

            lstrcpy (string, "File");
            mii.fMask = MIIM_TYPE | MIIM_SUBMENU;
            mii.hSubMenu = hMenu2;
            InsertMenuItem (hMenu, 0, FALSE,  &mii);

                HMENU hMenu2_;
                hMenu2_ = CreatePopupMenu ();
                lstrcpy (string, "Author");
                mii.fMask = MIIM_TYPE | MIIM_ID;
                mii.wID = 3;
                InsertMenuItem (hMenu2_, 0, FALSE,  &mii);
```

```
            HMENU hMenu3;
            hMenu3 = CreatePopupMenu ();
            lstrcpy (string, "Color depth");
            mii.fMask = MIIM_TYPE | MIIM_ID;
            mii.wID = 4;
            InsertMenuItem (hMenu3, 0, FALSE,  &mii);
            lstrcpy (string, "Resolution");
            mii.wID = 5;
            InsertMenuItem (hMenu3, 0, FALSE,  &mii);

            HMENU hMenu3_;

            hMenu3_ = CreatePopupMenu ();
            lstrcpy (string, "Windows directory");
            mii.wID = 6;
            InsertMenuItem (hMenu3_, 0, FALSE,  &mii);
            lstrcpy (string, "Current directory");
            mii.wID = 8;
            InsertMenuItem (hMenu3_, 0, FALSE,  &mii);

        lstrcpy (string, "Graphic");
        mii.fMask = MIIM_TYPE | MIIM_SUBMENU;
        mii.hSubMenu = hMenu3;
        InsertMenuItem (hMenu2_, 0, FALSE,  &mii);
        lstrcpy (string, "Hard disk");
        mii.hSubMenu = hMenu3_;
        InsertMenuItem (hMenu2_, 0, FALSE,  &mii);

    lstrcpy (string, "Information");
    mii.hSubMenu = hMenu2_;
    InsertMenuItem (hMenu, 0, FALSE,  &mii);


    SetMenu (hWnd, hMenu);

    delete string[];

    return 0;
case WM_COMMAND:
    if (HIWORD(wParam) == 0)
    {
     switch (LOWORD(wParam))
```

```
{
 case 1:
    HDC hdc;
    hdc = GetDC (hWnd);
    Rectangle (hdc, 10, 10, 100, 100);
    ReleaseDC(hWnd, hdc);
    return 0;
 case 2:
    DestroyWindow (hWnd);
    return 0;
 case 3:
    hdc = GetDC (hWnd);
    char *string1;
    string1 = new char[80];
    lstrcpy (string1, "Author: Henning Hansen");
    TextOut (hdc, 120, 10, string1,
             lstrlen(string1));
    ReleaseDC(hWnd, hdc);
    delete string1[];
    return 0;
 case 4:
    hdc = GetDC (hWnd);
    string1 = new char[80];
    lstrcpy (string1, "Color depth: ");
    int BitsPixel;
    BitsPixel = GetDeviceCaps (hdc, BITSPIXEL);
    char *string2;
    string2 = new char[80];
    itoa (BitsPixel, string2,10);
    lstrcat (string1, string2);
    TextOut (hdc, 120, 30, string1,
    lstrlen(string1));
    ReleaseDC(hWnd, hdc);
    delete string1[];
    delete string2[];
    return 0;
 case 5:
    hdc = GetDC (hWnd);
    string1 = new char[80];
    lstrcpy (string1, "Resolution: ");
    int HRes, VRes;
    HRes = GetDeviceCaps (hdc, HORZRES);
```

```
        string2 = new char[80];
        itoa (HRes, string2,10);
        lstrcat (string1, string2);
        lstrcat (string1, "x");
        VRes =  GetDeviceCaps (hdc, VERTRES)
        itoa (VRes, string2,10);
        lstrcat (string1, string2);
        TextOut (hdc, 120, 50, string1,
        lstrlen(string1));
        ReleaseDC(hWnd, hdc);
        delete string1[];
        delete string2[];
        return 0;
    case 6:
        hdc = GetDC (hWnd);
        string1 = new char[80];
        lstrcpy (string1, "Windows directory: ");
        string2 = new char[80];
        GetWindowsDirectory (string2, 500);
        lstrcat (string1, string2);
        TextOut (hdc, 120, 70, string1,
        lstrlen(string1));
        ReleaseDC(hWnd, hdc);
        delete string1[];
        delete string2[];
        return 0;
    case 8:
        hdc = GetDC (hWnd);
        string1 = new char[80];
        lstrcpy (string1,
                "Current directory:");
        string2 = new char[80];
        GetCurrentDirectory (500, string2);
        lstrcat (string1, string2);
        TextOut (hdc, 120, 90, string1,
                lstrlen(string1));
        ReleaseDC(hWnd, hdc);
        delete string1[];
        delete string2[];
        return 0;
    default:
        return 0;
```

```
            }

        }
        return 0;
    case WM_DESTROY:
        PostQuitMessage(0);
        return 0;
    default:
        return DefWindowProc (hWnd, uiMessage,
                              wParam, lParam);

    }

}
```

8.2.2 Explanation of the source code

The first part of the application contains what you already know. The changes and new features are in the window function, as is almost always the case. The first and most important changes relate to the WM_CREATE message handling function. The menu is created and assigned to the window there.

Creating the menu

This section describes how to create the menu. This involves creating menu objects and filling them with menu items. Some of these menu items are used as references to other menu objects. We then assign a menu object to the Windows window. This object is normally the highest object in the hierarchy so that it can be used to call all the other menu objects:

```
HMENU hMenu;
hMenu = CreateMenu ();
MENUITEMINFO mii;
mii.cbSize = sizeof(MENUITEMINFO);
mii.fMask = MIIM_TYPE | MIIM_ID;
mii.fType = MFT_STRING;
char *string;
string = new char[40];
lstrcpy (string,"Draw Box");
mii.dwTypeData = string;
mii.cch = lstrlen (string);
mii.fState = MFS_ENABLED;
mii.wID = 1;
InsertMenuItem (hMenu, 0, FALSE,  &mii);
```

```
                          HMENU hMenu2;
                          hMenu2 = CreatePopupMenu ();
                          lstrcpy (string, "Exit");
                          mii.wID = 2;
                          InsertMenuItem (hMenu2, 0, FALSE,  &mii);

                     lstrcpy (string, "File");
                     mii.fMask = MIIM_TYPE | MIIM_SUBMENU;
                     mii.hSubMenu = hMenu2;
                     InsertMenuItem (hMenu, 0, FALSE,  &mii);

                          HMENU hMenu2_;
                          hMenu2_ = CreatePopupMenu ();
                          lstrcpy (string, "Author");
                          mii.fMask = MIIM_TYPE | MIIM_ID;
                          mii.wID = 3;
                          InsertMenuItem (hMenu2_, 0, FALSE,  &mii);

                             HMENU hMenu3;
                             hMenu3 = CreatePopupMenu ();
                             lstrcpy (string, "Color depth");
                             mii.fMask = MIIM_TYPE | MIIM_ID;
                             mii.wID = 4;
                             InsertMenuItem (hMenu3, 0, FALSE,  &mii);
                             lstrcpy (string, "Resolution");
                             mii.wID = 5;
                             InsertMenuItem (hMenu3, 0, FALSE,  &mii);

                             HMENU hMenu3_;
                             hMenu3_ = CreatePopupMenu ();
                             lstrcpy (string, "Windows directory");
                             mii.wID = 6;
                             InsertMenuItem (hMenu3_, 0, FALSE,  &mii);
                             lstrcpy (string, "Current directory");
                             mii.wID = 8;
                             InsertMenuItem (hMenu3_, 0, FALSE,  &mii);

                          lstrcpy (string, "Graphic");
                          mii.fMask = MIIM_TYPE | MIIM_SUBMENU;
                          mii.hSubMenu = hMenu3;
                          InsertMenuItem (hMenu2_, 0, FALSE,  &mii);
                          lstrcpy (string, "Hard disk");
```

```
        mii.hSubMenu = hMenu3_;
        InsertMenuItem (hMenu2_, 0, FALSE,  &mii);


    lstrcpy (string, "Information");
    mii.hSubMenu = hMenu2_;
    InsertMenuItem (hMenu, 0, FALSE,  &mii);



    SetMenu (hWnd, hMenu);


    delete string[];
```

The highest menu in the hierarchy

A variable of the type HMENU is created. This is a handle to a menu object. The menu object is then created and the handle to the object is passed to the variable. We do this using the CreateMenu function:

```
HMENU CreateMenu(VOID);
```

The function looks almost exactly the same in the source code:

```
hMenu = CreateMenu ();
```

→ The function has no parameters. Only a handle to a menu object is returned.

Adding entries to the menu

We use the InsertMenuItem function to insert entries in the menu object:

```
BOOL WINAPI InsertMenuItem( HMENU hMenu, UINT uItem,
                            BOOL fByPosition,
                            LPMENUITEMINFO lpmii);
```

This function is used several times in the source code:

```
        InsertMenuItem (hMenu, 0, FALSE,  &mii);
          InsertMenuItem (hMenu2, 0, FALSE,  &mii);
        InsertMenuItem (hMenu, 0, FALSE,  &mii);
          InsertMenuItem (hMenu2_, 0, FALSE,  &mii);
            InsertMenuItem (hMenu3, 0, FALSE,  &mii);
            InsertMenuItem (hMenu3, 0, FALSE,  &mii);
            InsertMenuItem (hMenu3_, 0, FALSE,  &mii);
            InsertMenuItem (hMenu3_, 0, FALSE,  &mii);
          InsertMenuItem (hMenu2_, 0, FALSE,  &mii);
          InsertMenuItem (hMenu2_, 0, FALSE,  &mii);
        InsertMenuItem (hMenu, 0, FALSE,  &mii);
```

→ hMenu is the handle to the menu object to which you want to write the item.

→ uItem is either an ID number for the menu item or a position at which the menu item is to appear. The next parameter determines whether the value is used for identification or to specify a position. This value is set to FALSE because it is not needed.

→ fByPosition is of the type BOOL and can therefore only be TRUE or FALSE. If this is FALSE, the uItem value is an identifier, but if it is TRUE, it is a value that specifies the position of the menu item. We set this value to 0 because it is not needed.

→ And finally, we have a pointer to a structure of the type MENUITEMINFO. This structure contains further information, which is passed on to the menu item.

The MENUITEMINFO structure is used not only by the InsertMenuItem command, but also by other commands. It can be used to set and request the properties of a menu item:

```
typedef struct tagMENUITEMINFO
{
    UINT    cbSize;
    UINT    fMask;
    UINT    fType;
    UINT    fState;
    UINT    wID;
    HMENU   hSubMenu;
    HBITMAP hbmpChecked;
    HBITMAP hbmpUnchecked;
    DWORD   dwItemData;
    LPTSTR  dwTypeData;
    UINT    cch;
} MENUITEMINFO, FAR *LPMENUITEMINFO;
```

→ cbSize is the size of the structure in bytes.

→ `fMask` comprises a number of constants and specifies which data is to be retrieved or set.

   `MIIM_ID` means that an ID is to be set for the menu item, or that the value of the menu item is to be retrieved.
   `MIIM_TYPE` means that the value of `fType` and `dwTypeData` is to be set or retrieved.
   `MIIM_SUBMENU` means that the value of `hSubMenu` is to be set or retrieved.

→ `fType` provides information about which property is defined for the menu item. For example, the menu item may be a text string, a dividing line or a bitmap.
   `MFT_STRING` means that the menu item is a text string.

→ `fState` provides information about the status of menu items. This is only required if the menu item has a check box, for example, or if it cannot be clicked.

→ `wID` is a value that represents the menu item's identifier.

→ `hSubMenu` is the handle to a menu object. This handle is linked to the menu item. This value must be set if the menu item refers to a submenu object.

→ `hBmpChecked` is the handle to a bitmap object, which is to be displayed when the menu item is checked.

→ `hBmpUnChecked` is the handle to the bitmap if it is not checked.

→ `dwItemData` is a value defined by the application.

→ `dwTypeData` contains a pointer to the data that was set by `fType`.

→ `cch` specifies the length of the menu item text, if this is required.

Assigning the menu to the window

Once you have created the entire menu hierarchy, you must now assign the menu to the window using the `SetMenu` command:

```
BOOL SetMenu( HWND hWnd, HMENU hMenu);
```

This function is assigned to the menu creation function at the end:

```
SetMenu (hWnd, hMenu);
```

→ `hWnd` is the handle to the window object to which you want to assign the menu.

→ `hMenu` is the handle to the menu object that is assigned to the window object.

Executing menu actions

You use the WM_COMMAND message to do this. When you click a menu item, WM_COMMAND is inserted into the application's queue:

```
WM_COMMAND
wNotifyCode = HIWORD(wParam);
wID = LOWORD(wParam);
hwndCtl = (HWND) lParam;
```

➜ wNotifyCode always has the value 0 for a message from a menu item.
➜ wID is the ID of the menu item. It corresponds to the value that was transferred in the MENUITEMINFO structure.
➜ hwndCtl is always NULL for menu messages.

The evaluation in the window function is then performed based on this data. A number of actions then start. We will now take a closer look at the new main commands for these actions.

Device context information

You can use the GetDeviceCaps function to obtain information about the device contexts, i.e. about certain devices in the system. These devices may be a graphics card, printer or camera, for example:

```
int GetDeviceCaps( HDC hdc, int nIndex);
```

This function appears several times in the source code:

```
BitsPixel = GetDeviceCaps (hdc, BITSPIXEL);
HRes = GetDeviceCaps (hdc, HORZRES);
VRes =  GetDeviceCaps (hdc, VERTRES);
```

➜ hdc is the handle to the device context object. This device context object is linked to a device, which is used to retrieve the information.
➜ nIndex requests a constant, which indicates which value is to be returned.
➜ The value containing information about the device is supplied as the return value.

Determining directories

There are two kinds of directories that you can determine by default. These include the Windows directory, the system directory and the current directory. The Windows directory is the directory that was defined when Windows was installed. It contains Windows applications, initialization files and help files. The system directory contains DLL, driver and font files. As a rule, it is defined in the Windows directory with the name System. The current directory is different for every application and is the directory from which the application was started, unless it was changed afterwards.

The `GetWindowsDirectory` function determines the Windows directory:

```
UINT GetWindowsDirectory( LPTSTR lpBuffer, UINT uSize);
```

This function is used once in the source code:

```
GetWindowsDirectory (string2, 500);
```

→ `lpBuffer` is a pointer of the type `char`.
→ `uSize` is the size of the array to which `lpBuffer` points.

The `GetCurrentDirectory` function determines the current directory:

```
DWORD GetCurrentDirectory( DWORD nBufferLength,
                           LPTSTR lpBuffer);
```

It appears once in the source code:

```
GetCurrentDirectory (500, string2);
```

→ `nBufferLength` is the size of the array to which the next parameter points.
→ `lpBuffer` is a pointer of the type `char`.

Handling files 9

9.1 General information

9.1.1   File systems

There are a number of file systems that are supported by various Windows versions. For example, Windows NT supports the NTFS and Windows 95/98 supports the "Protected FAT File System". These file systems define how files and directories are stored on the hard disk. This includes information like the length of file names, which characters a file name can contain or which security attributes are set for the files.

9.1.2   Functions

Windows provides functions for accessing these file systems. These functions run under all the file systems. This means that the code that was written for a program for Windows 95 can be executed correctly in Windows NT. File management also works in the same way.

9.2 An application

9.2.1   The source code

The following application is an editor, which is screen-based only (see Figure 9.1). It has a menu. You can close the editor by selecting the "Exit" menu item. The New function sets the character buffer to 0 characters. You can then enter new text (see Figure 9.2). The "Save" function saves the text from the edit field – the main component of the editor – to the file C:\TEXT.TXT. You can use the "Open" function to open the existing C:\TEXT.TXT file. This incorporates the most important file functions into the program.

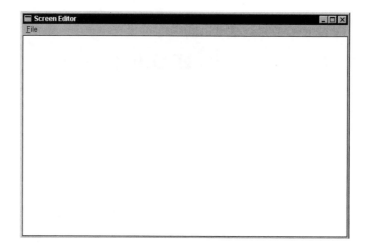

Figure 9.1 *The application after you start it*

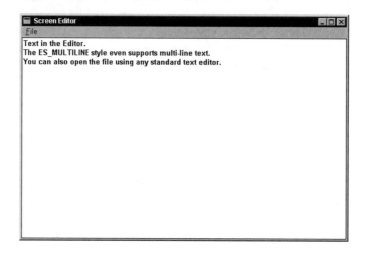

Figure 9.2 *The application with sample text*

```
#include <windows.h>

LRESULT CALLBACK WndProc (HWND, UINT, WPARAM, LPARAM);


HINSTANCE hInstGlobal;
HWND hEdit;

int APIENTRY WinMain(HINSTANCE hInstance,
```

```
                   HINSTANCE hPrevInstance,
                   LPSTR     lpCmdLine,
                   int       nCmdShow )
{


   hInstGlobal = hInstance;


   WNDCLASS WndClass;
   WndClass.style = 0;
   WndClass.cbClsExtra = 0;
   WndClass.cbWndExtra = 0;
   WndClass.lpfnWndProc = WndProc;
   WndClass.hInstance = hInstance;
   WndClass.hbrBackground = (HBRUSH) (COLOR_WINDOW+1);
   WndClass.hCursor = LoadCursor (NULL, IDC_ARROW);
   WndClass.hIcon = LoadIcon (NULL, IDI_APPLICATION);
   WndClass.lpszMenuName = 0;
   WndClass.lpszClassName = "WinProg";


   RegisterClass(&WndClass);


   HWND hWindow;
   hWindow = CreateWindow("WinProg","Screen Editor",
                      WS_OVERLAPPEDWINDOW,
                      0,0,600,400,NULL,NULL,
                      hInstance, NULL);


   ShowWindow (hWindow, nCmdShow);


   UpdateWindow (hWindow);


   MSG Message;
   while (GetMessage(&Message, NULL, 0, 0))


   {
      TranslateMessage (&Message);
      DispatchMessage(&Message);
   }


   return (Message.wParam);
}
```

```
LRESULT CALLBACK WndProc (HWND hWnd, UINT uiMessage,
                          WPARAM wParam,LPARAM lParam)
{
    switch(uiMessage)
    {
        case WM_CREATE:
            HMENU hMenu;
            hMenu = CreateMenu ();
            MENUITEMINFO mii;
            mii.cbSize = sizeof(MENUITEMINFO);
            mii.fMask = MIIM_TYPE | MIIM_ID;
            mii.fType = MFT_STRING;
            char *string;
            string = new char[40];
            mii.dwTypeData = string;
            mii.cch = lstrlen (string);

            HMENU hMenu2;
            hMenu2 = CreatePopupMenu ();

            lstrcpy (string, "&New");
            mii.dwTypeData = string;
            mii.cch = lstrlen (string);
            mii.wID = 1;
            InsertMenuItem (hMenu2, 1, TRUE,  &mii);

            lstrcpy (string, "&Open c:\\text.txt");
            mii.dwTypeData = string;
            mii.cch = lstrlen (string);
            mii.wID = 2;
            InsertMenuItem (hMenu2, 2, TRUE,  &mii);

            lstrcpy (string, "&Save c:\\text.txt");
            mii.dwTypeData = string;
            mii.cch = lstrlen (string);
            mii.wID = 3;
            InsertMenuItem (hMenu2, 3, TRUE,  &mii);

            mii.fMask = MIIM_TYPE;
            mii.fType = MFT_SEPARATOR;
            InsertMenuItem (hMenu2, 4, TRUE,  &mii);
```

```
        mii.fMask = MIIM_TYPE | MIIM_ID;
        mii.fType = MFT_STRING;
        lstrcpy (string, "E&xit");
        mii.dwTypeData = string;
        mii.cch = lstrlen (string);
        mii.wID = 4;
        InsertMenuItem (hMenu2, 5, TRUE,  &mii);


     lstrcpy (string, "&File");
     mii.dwTypeData = string;
     mii.cch = lstrlen (string);
     mii.fMask = MIIM_TYPE | MIIM_SUBMENU;
     mii.hSubMenu = hMenu2;
     InsertMenuItem (hMenu, 1, FALSE,  &mii);


     SetMenu (hWnd, hMenu);


     RECT rect;
     GetClientRect (hWnd, &rect);
     hEdit = CreateWindow("EDIT","",
                     WS_CHILD | WS_VISIBLE |
                     WS_BORDER | ES_MULTILINE,
                     0,0,rect.right,rect.bottom,
                     hWnd,(HMENU) 1,
                     hInstGlobal, NULL);
     return 0;

case WM_SIZE:
   GetClientRect (hWnd, &rect);
   MoveWindow (hEdit, 0, 0, rect.right,
             rect.bottom,TRUE);
   return 0;
case WM_COMMAND:
   if (HIWORD(wParam) == 0)
   {
    switch LOWORD(wParam)
    {
     case 1:
        char *EditString;
        EditString = new char[80];
        lstrcpy (EditString, "");
        SetWindowText (hEdit, EditString);
```

```
                delete [] Editstring;
                return 0;
            case 2:
                HANDLE hFile;
                hFile = CreateFile ("c:\\text.txt",
                                    GENERIC_READ, 0,
                                    NULL, OPEN_EXISTING,
                                    NULL, NULL);
                DWORD Size;
                Size = GetFileSize (hFile, NULL);
                char *FileText;
                FileText = new char[Size+1];
                DWORD Readd;
                ReadFile (hFile, FileText, Size+1,
                          &Readd, NULL);
                CloseHandle (hFile);
                SetWindowText (hEdit, FileText);
                delete [] Editstring;
                return 0;
            case 3:
                hFile = CreateFile ("c:\\text.txt",
                                    GENERIC_WRITE, 0, NULL,
                                    CREATE_ALWAYS,
                                    NULL, NULL);
                FileText = new char[GetWindowTextLength(
                                    hEdit)+1];
                GetWindowText (hEdit, FileText,
                               GetWindowTextLength(
                                        hEdit)+1);
                WriteFile (hFile, FileText,
                           GetWindowTextLength(hEdit)+1,
                           &Readd, NULL);
                CloseHandle (hFile);
                delete [] FileText;
                return 0;
            case 4:
                PostQuitMessage (0);
                return 0;
            }
        }
        return 0;
    case WM_DESTROY:
```

```
        PostQuitMessage(0);
        return 0;
    default:
        return DefWindowProc (hWnd, uiMessage,
                                wParam, lParam);
    }
}
```

9.2.2   Explanation of the source code

Since the application essentially contains elements that you already know, we will concentrate on the file functions.

Opening a file or creating a new file

When you click the FILE/OPEN function in the menu, the application either opens an existing file or creates a new one. The data for this file is read into a buffer. A file object, which you must then close again, is created for this purpose so that other programs can also access this file. The data that was read in is then transferred to the edit field:

```
case 2:
    HANDLE hFile;
    hFile = CreateFile ("c:\\text.txt",
                        GENERIC_READ,0,
                        NULL,OPEN_EXISTING,
                        NULL,NULL);
    DWORD Size;
    Size = GetFileSize (hFile, NULL);
    char *FileText;
    FileText = new char[Size+1];
    DWORD Readd;
    ReadFile (hFile,FileText,Size+1,
            &Readd,NULL);
    CloseHandle (hFile);
    SetWindowText (hEdit, FileText);
    return 0;
```

CreateFile

The CreateFile function creates a file object and returns a handle to this file object:

```
HANDLE CreateFile( LPCTSTR lpFileName,
                   DWORD dwDesiredAccess,
                   DWORD dwShareMode,
                   LPSECURITY_ATTRIBUTES
                   lpSecurityAttributes,
                   DWORD dwCreationDisposition,
                   DWORD dwFlagsAndAttributes,
                   HANDLE hTemplateFile);
```

This function is used in the source code to open or create a new file, on the one hand, or to create a file for saving data, on the other:

```
hFile = CreateFile ("c:\\text.txt",
                    GENERIC_READ,0,
                    NULL,OPEN_EXISTING,
                    NULL,NULL);
hFile = CreateFile ("c:\\text.txt",
                    GENERIC_WRITE,0,NULL,
                    CREATE_ALWAYS,
                    NULL,NULL);
```

→ lpFileName is a pointer to an array of the type char. You must enter the name and path of the file here.

→ dwDesiredAccess indicates the type of access to the object in question. Two types are needed for accessing a file:

GENERIC_READ sets read access for the file.
GENERIC_WRITE sets write access for the file.

→ dwSharedMode indicates whether the object can be accessed a number of times simultaneously. This value is set to 0 so that shared access is not possible.

→ lpSecurityAttributes is a pointer to a SECURITY_ATTRIBUTES structure. This structure contains information about this object's inheritance and its access rights in Windows NT. This value is set to NULL. This means that the object cannot be inherited.

→ dwCreationDisposition provides further information for the action that was set using dwDesiredAccess.

OPEN_EXISTING means that only existing files are to be opened when accessed.

CREATE_ALWAYS indicates that a new file is created even if the file already exists.

→ dwFlagsAndAttributes sets the file attributes for user access and server/client access. This value is set to NULL.

→ hTemplateFile is set to NULL. We will not discuss the meaning of this parameter in detail here.

ReadFile

The ReadFile function reads data from a file into a buffer:

```
BOOL ReadFile( HANDLE hFile,
               LPVOID lpBuffer,
               DWORD nNumberOfBytesToRead,
               LPDWORD lpNumberOfBytesRead,
               LPOVERLAPPED lpOverlapped);
```

This function is used once in the source code to read a file:

```
ReadFile (hFile,FileText,Size+1,
          &Readd,NULL);
```

→ hFile is the handle to the file object.
→ lpBuffer is a pointer to a buffer.
→ nNumberOfBytesToRead is the number of bytes to be read from the file.
→ lpNumberOfBytesRead is the number of bytes read. Since this value is returned, it must be specified as a pointer.
→ lpOverlapped instructs the application to read a file, starting from a certain offset. This value is set to NULL. As a result, the file is always read from the start of the file.

WriteFile

The WriteFile function writes data from a buffer into a file object:

```
BOOL WriteFile( HANDLE hFile,
                LPCVOID lpBuffer,
                DWORD nNumberOfBytesToWrite
                LPDWORD lpNumberOfBytesWritten,
                LPOVERLAPPED lpOverlapped);
```

This function is used once in the source code. Every function with file access generally changes the data directly in the file:

```
WriteFile (hFile,FileText,
           GetWindowTextLength(hEdit)+1,
              S&Readd,NULL);
```

→ hFile is the handle to the file object to which the data from the buffer is to be written.

→ lpBuffer is a pointer to the buffer.

→ nNumberOfBytesToWrite is the number of bytes to be written from the buffer into the file object.

→ lpNumberOfBytesWritten specifies the number of bytes that have actually been written to the file object.

→ lpOverlapped specifies the offset. This value has the same meaning as the value used in ReadFile.

CloseHandle

You can use the CloseHandle function to remove a file object:

```
BOOL CloseHandle( HANDLE hObject);
```

This function is called once to close the file object for read access and once for write access:

```
CloseHandle (hFile);
```

→ hFile is the handle to the file object to be closed.

Applications, processes and threads

10.1 General information

An *application* is the EXE file on the hard disk. It contains all the data.

A *process* is the application when it is run. For example, a number of processes of the same application can run on a system at any one time.

*Thread*s are used to execute the code in the application. They tell the system where to find the next command to be run. You can create several threads for one process. We call this multi-threading. For example, you use multi-threading if you are working with a very time-consuming data structure. While this data structure is being processed, the user must be able to move the window and even cancel data processing, if necessary. To do this, you then use a separate thread, which only performs data processing. A very important point to note here is that every thread has its own queue for messages. This means that the previous explanations of the applications were highly simplified in order to concentrate initially on the most fundamental aspects.

10.2 A multi-threading application

10.2.1 The source code

The following application creates a window (see Figure 10.1). We still want to carry out message processing. At the same time, we want to start an operation that is very time-consuming. We will create a thread to perform this operation. This operation is a loop that continually draws new boxes (see Figure 10.2). The window can be moved or reduced in size during this operation.

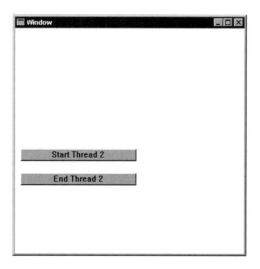

Figure 10.1 *The application after you start it*

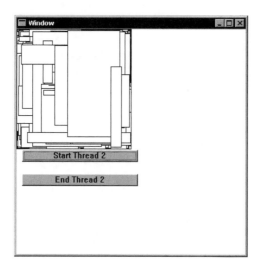

Figure 10.2 *The application after you start thread 2*

```
#include <windows.h>

LRESULT CALLBACK WndProc (HWND, UINT, WPARAM, LPARAM);
DWORD WINAPI ThreadProc ( LPVOID);

int APIENTRY WinMain(HINSTANCE hInstance,
                     HINSTANCE hPrevInstance,
```

```
                    LPSTR      lpCmdLine,
                    int        nCmdShow )
{

    WNDCLASS WndClass;
    WndClass.style = 0;
    WndClass.cbClsExtra = 0;
    WndClass.cbWndExtra = 0;
    WndClass.lpfnWndProc = WndProc;
    WndClass.hInstance = hInstance;
    WndClass.hbrBackground = (HBRUSH) (COLOR_WINDOW+1);
    WndClass.hCursor = LoadCursor (NULL, IDC_ARROW);
    WndClass.hIcon = LoadIcon (NULL, IDI_APPLICATION);
    WndClass.lpszMenuName = 0;
    WndClass.lpszClassName = "WinProg";

    RegisterClass(&WndClass);

HWND hWindow,hButton;

    hWindow = CreateWindow("WinProg","Window",
                    WS_OVERLAPPEDWINDOW,
                    0,0,400,400,NULL,NULL,
                    hInstance, NULL);

    hButton = CreateWindow("BUTTON","Start Thread 2",
                    WS_CHILD | WS_VISIBLE
                    | BS_PUSHBUTTON,
                    10,200,200,20,hWindow,
                    (HMENU) 1, hInstance, NULL);

    hButton = CreateWindow("BUTTON","End Thread 2",
                    WS_CHILD | WS_VISIBLE
                    | BS_PUSHBUTTON,
                    10,240,200,20,hWindow,
                    (HMENU) 2, hInstance, NULL);

    ShowWindow (hWindow, nCmdShow);

    UpdateWindow (hWindow);
```

```
    MSG Message;
    while (GetMessage(&Message, NULL, 0, 0))
    {
        DispatchMessage(&Message);
    }

    return (Message.wParam);
}


DWORD WINAPI ThreadProc( LPVOID pvoid )
{
 int value = 2;
 while (value == 2)
 {
  HDC hdc1;
  hdc1 = GetDC (hWindow);
  Rectangle (hdc1, border()%200, border()%200 ,
             border()%200, border()%200);
  ReleaseDC (hWindow, hdc1);
 }
}


LRESULT CALLBACK WndProc (HWND hWnd, UINT uiMessage,
                          WPARAM wParam,LPARAM lParam)
{
    static HANDLE hThread;


    switch(uiMessage)

        case WM_COMMAND:
            if (HIWORD(wParam) == BN_CLICKED)
            {
             if (LOWORD(wParam) == 1)
             {
              DWORD dwThreadParam = 1;
              DWORD dwThreadID;
              hThread = CreateThread (NULL, 0, ThreadProc,
                                      &dwThreadParam, 0,
                                      &dwThreadID);
```

```
      }
      if (LOWORD(wParam) == 2)
      {
       TerminateThread (hThread, 0);
      }
      }
      return 0;
   case WM_DESTROY:
      PostQuitMessage(0);
      return 0;
   default:
      return DefWindowProc (hWnd, uiMessage,
                            wParam, lParam);
   }
}
```

10.2.2   Explanation of the source code

This program creates the new thread, which draws in the window while the first thread of the process continues to process messages. Since each thread has its own message processing queue, all the messages for the windows that are already created are assigned to the message queue belonging to the other thread.

The CreateThread function creates the new thread and assigns a function to it:

```
HANDLE CreateThread( LPSECURITY_ATTRIBUTES
                     lpThreadAttributes,
                     DWORD dwStackSize,
                     LPTHREAD_START_ROUTINE
                     lpStartAddress,
                     LPVOID lpParameter,
                     DWORD dwCreationFlags,
                     LPDWORD lpThreadId);
```

This function is used in the following way in the source code:

```
hThread = CreateThread (NULL, 0, ThreadProc,
                        &dwThreadParam, 0,
                        &dwThreadID);
```

→ lpThreadAttributes forms a structure of the type
  SECURITY_ATTRIBUTES, which defines certain security regulations for
  the thread. This value is simply set to NULL so that the handle cannot be
  inherited.

➜ dwStackSize is the size of the stack during initialization. If this is set to NULL, the stack size defined for the calling thread is also used here.

➜ lpStartAddress is a pointer to the start of the function, which the thread executes.

➜ lpParameter is a 32-bit value that is passed on to the thread. This value is transferred to the function, which the thread executes. It must be transferred as a pointer.

➜ dwCreationFlags is a value that is defined by certain constants. The thread can be initialized in such a way that it is not executed (*suspended*), or with a value indicating that the thread is to be executed as soon as it has been created.

➜ lpThreadID is a pointer to a 32-bit value containing an identifier for the thread.

➜ This function supplies the value of the handle to the thread object as the return value.

The TerminateThread function deletes the thread so that the function code is no longer executed:

```
BOOL TerminateThread( HANDLE hThread, DWORD dwExitCode);
```

You can call this function by clicking the button with the code 2:

```
TerminateThread (hThread, 0);
```

➜ hThread is the handle to the thread object to be deleted.

➜ dwExitCode is the exit code for the thread.

DLL files

11.1 General information

You can incorporate library files containing the entire code into C++ (e.g. `Stdlib.lib`). This means that every program has all the code for the library files stored in memory. Microsoft invented the DLL files (*Dynamic Link Library*) in order to prevent this. You include the header files and library files in the program as before, but the code for the individual functions is no longer contained in the library files but in DLL files. Only references to the code in the DLL files are incorporated into the program. And only one DLL file, which is used by all the programs, must be stored in memory. If the relevant file is not yet in the memory, it is loaded. You can also load DLL files directly from the program's source code. DLL files have many advantages – for example, using a DLL requires less memory and we can also update one or more applications by simply modifying the DLL.

The entire Win32 API was designed as a collection of DLL files.

A DLL file contains functions and data. These functions and data are either internal or external. Internal means that the functions and data are only used by functions in the DLL file. External means that the functions and data are used by a program.

DLL files are used in different ways, e.g. they can be used as "load-time dynamic link files". These files are loaded when you start the program and are then stored in the virtual address space of the process. The process code is changed in such a way that the DLL functions are called. The change is made using the information from the library file. DLL files are also used as "runtime dynamic link" files. You can load a DLL file using `LoadLibrary` and find out the addresses of the functions in the DLL file using the `GetProcAddress` function. These addresses are used to call the functions.

We will only discuss the load-time dynamic link files in this chapter.

11.2 An application

11.2.1 The source code

The following DLL file provides a function. This function simply draws a box in a device context handle that was transferred (see Figures 11.1 and 11.2). A LIB file is also created when you create a DLL file. This LIB file contains references to the functions in the DLL file. You must write the header file yourself, however. It is intended for the creation process:

```
#include <windows.h>
#include "Rectangle.h"

int WINAPI DllMain (HINSTANCE hInstance, DWORD fdwReason,
                    PVOID pvReserved)
{
   return TRUE;
}


__declspec ( dllexport ) BOOL CALLBACK Rectangle (HDC hdc)
{
   Rectangle (hdc, 10, 10, 200, 200);
   return 0;
}
```

The header file looks like this:

```
__declspec ( dllexport ) BOOL CALLBACK Rectangle (HDC);
```

Once you have created the DLL file, you must incorporate the header file and the LIB file into the source code.

Figure 11.1 *The application after you start it*

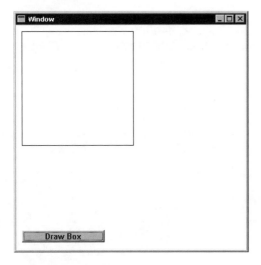

Figure 11.2 *The application after using the DLL file*

The actual program contains the following source code:

```
#include <windows.h>
#include "Rectangle.h"

LRESULT CALLBACK WndProc (HWND, UINT, WPARAM, LPARAM);

int APIENTRY WinMain(HINSTANCE hInstance,
                     HINSTANCE hPrevInstance,
```

```
                          LPSTR      lpCmdLine,
                          int        nCmdShow )
{
    WNDCLASS WndClass;
    WndClass.style = 0;
    WndClass.cbClsExtra = 0;
    WndClass.cbWndExtra = 0;
    WndClass.lpfnWndProc = WndProc;
    WndClass.hInstance = hInstance;
    WndClass.hbrBackground = (HBRUSH) (COLOR_WINDOW+1);
    WndClass.hCursor = LoadCursor (NULL, IDC_ARROW);
    WndClass.hIcon = LoadIcon (NULL, IDI_APPLICATION);
    WndClass.lpszMenuName = 0;
    WndClass.lpszClassName = "WinProg";

    RegisterClass(&WndClass);

    HWND hWindow,hButton;
    hWindow = CreateWindow("WinProg","Window",
                        WS_OVERLAPPEDWINDOW,
                        0,0,400,400,NULL,NULL,
                        hInstance, NULL);
    hButton = CreateWindow("BUTTON","Draw Box",
                        WS_CHILD | WS_VISIBLE
                        | BS_PUSHBUTTON,
                        10,340,140,20,hWindow,(HMENU) 1,
                        hInstance, NULL);

    ShowWindow (hWindow, nCmdShow);

    UpdateWindow (hWindow);

    MSG Message;
    while (GetMessage(&Message, NULL, 0, 0))
    {
        DispatchMessage(&Message);
    }

    return (Message.wParam);
}

LRESULT CALLBACK WndProc (HWND hWnd, UINT uiMessage,
```

```
                    WPARAM wParam,LPARAM lParam)
{
   switch(uiMessage)
   {
      case WM_COMMAND:
         if (HIWORD(wParam) == BN_CLICKED)
         {
          if (LOWORD(wParam) == 1)
          {
           HDC hdc;
           hdc = GetDC (hWnd);
           Rectangle (hdc);
           ReleaseDC (hWnd, hdc);
          }
         }
         return 0;
      case WM_DESTROY:
         PostQuitMessage(0);
         return 0;
      default:
         return DefWindowProc (hWnd, uiMessage,
                               wParam, lParam);
   }
}
```

11.2.2   Explanation of the source code

Creating a DLL file

The same principles that apply to the creation of a LIB file are also relevant for creating a DLL file. You create its functions in the usual way. You set up references to these functions from the header file. You then use a program to develop the DLL file and a LIB file. But this time, the LIB file only contains references to the functions in the DLL file. Later, you will call the functions in the same way as if you had created a normal LIB file.

The DllMain function

The DllMain function is called when a program reinitializes the file or no longer needs it. This function is optional and supplies three parameters.

```
int WINAPI DllMain (HINSTANCE hInstance, DWORD fdwReason,
                    PVOID pvReserved)
```

→ hInstance is a handle to the DLL. The value of the handle is the base address of the DLL file in the memory.

→ fdwReason is a value that determines whether the DLL file was loaded into the virtual address space or if it is to be removed from the virtual address space. The constants DLL_PROCESS_ATTACH (load) and DLL_PROCESS_DETACH (remove) describe both these options. There are also other situations in which the DllMain function is called.

A standard function for a DLL file

Functions in a DLL file are defined in almost exactly the same way as the functions in a LIB file. This ensures that the functions are visible externally and that they can also be called using different languages.

This function draws a box in a transferred device context handle. Of course, you don't need a DLL file for that.

```
__declspec ( dllexport ) BOOL CALLBACK Rectangle (HDC hdc)
{
    Rectangle (hdc, 10, 10, 200, 200);
    return 0;
}
```

The header file

The function name is mentioned once again – as usual – in the header file.

```
__declspec ( dllexport ) BOOL CALLBACK Rectangle (HDC);
```

The program for calling the DLL file

You call a DLL LIB file in the same way as a normal LIB file, but you must make sure that the DLL file is loaded into memory. You must incorporate the header file and that's about all we need to say about the program. You can now use the function in the usual way.

Timers

12.1 General information

A timer calls a function at certain time intervals. It can also send a WM_TIMER message to a window at certain time intervals. Timers are managed by the system.

12.2 An application with timer messages

12.2.1 The source code

This application creates a timer, which sends messages to the window at certain time intervals. Two counters XPos and YPos are defined. These two counters specify the new position and size of the window. The window continually changes its position and size (see Figures 12.1 and 12.2).

Figure 12.1 *The application a certain time after you start it*

Figure 12.2 *The application after more time has elapsed*

```c
#include <windows.h>

int XPos, YPos;


LRESULT CALLBACK WndProc (HWND, UINT, WPARAM, LPARAM);

int APIENTRY WinMain(HINSTANCE hInstance,
                     HINSTANCE hPrevInstance,
                     LPSTR     lpCmdLine,
                     int       nCmdShow )
{
   XPos = 0;
   YPos = 0;
   WNDCLASS WndClass;
   WndClass.style = 0;
   WndClass.cbClsExtra = 0;
   WndClass.cbWndExtra = 0;
   WndClass.lpfnWndProc = WndProc;
   WndClass.hInstance = hInstance;
   WndClass.hbrBackground = (HBRUSH) (COLOR_WINDOW+1);
   WndClass.hCursor = LoadCursor (NULL, IDC_ARROW);
   WndClass.hIcon = LoadIcon (NULL, IDI_APPLICATION);
   WndClass.lpszMenuName = 0;
   WndClass.lpszClassName = "WinProg";

   RegisterClass(&WndClass);
```

```
HWND hWindow,hButton,hButtonExit;
hWindow = CreateWindow("WinProg","Window",
                    WS_OVERLAPPEDWINDOW,
                    XPos,YPos,
                    400-XPos,400-YPos,NULL,NULL,
                    hInstance, NULL);
hButtonExit = CreateWindow("BUTTON","Exit",
                    WS_CHILD | WS_VISIBLE |
                    BS_PUSHBUTTON,
                    0,0,140,20,hWindow,(HMENU) 2,
                    hInstance, NULL);

ShowWindow (hWindow, nCmdShow);

UpdateWindow (hWindow);
SetTimer (hWindow, 1, 10, NULL);

MSG Message;
while (GetMessage(&Message, NULL, 0, 0))
{
    DispatchMessage(&Message);
}

return (Message.wParam);
}


LRESULT CALLBACK WndProc (HWND hWnd, UINT uiMessage,
                        WPARAM wParam,LPARAM lParam)
{
    switch(uiMessage)
    {
        case WM_COMMAND:

            DestroyWindow (hWnd);
            return 0;
        case WM_TIMER:
            if (XPos < 200)
            {
             XPos++;
            }
```

```
      else
      {
       XPos = 0;
      }
      if (YPos < 40)
      {
       YPos = YPos + 4;
      }
      else
      {
       YPos = 0;
      }
      SetWindowPos (hWnd, HWND_TOP, XPos, YPos,
                    400-(XPos*2), 400-(YPos*2),
                    SWP_SHOWWINDOW);
      return 0;
    case WM_DESTROY:
      PostQuitMessage(0);
      return 0;
    default:
      return DefWindowProc (hWnd, uiMessage,
                            wParam, lParam);

  }
}
```

12.2.2   Explanation of the source code

SetTimer

The SetTimer function is used here to send WM_TIMER to a window at certain time intervals:

```
UINT SetTimer( HWND hWnd, UINT nIDEvent,
               UINT uElapse, TIMERPROC lpTimerFunc);
```

→ hWnd is the handle to the window to which the WM_TIMER message is to be sent.

→ nIDEvent is a value that is used to identify timer messages, if a number of timers exist.

→ uElapse is the time in milliseconds that it takes to send the WM_TIMER messages.

→ lpTimerFunc is set to NULL so that messages are only sent to one window.

12.3 An application with a timer function

12.3.1 The source code

This application does the same as the first timer application. It does not send timer messages, however, but executes a timer function at certain time intervals:

```c
#include <windows.h>

int XPos, YPos;
HWND hWindow;

LRESULT CALLBACK WndProc (HWND, UINT, WPARAM, LPARAM);
VOID CALLBACK TimerProc(HWND, UINT, UINT, DWORD);

int APIENTRY WinMain(HINSTANCE hInstance,
                     HINSTANCE hPrevInstance
                     LPSTR     lpCmdLine,
                     int       nCmdShow )
{
   XPos = 0;
   YPos = 0;

   WNDCLASS WndClass;
   WndClass.style = 0;
   WndClass.cbClsExtra = 0;
   WndClass.cbWndExtra = 0;
   WndClass.lpfnWndProc = WndProc;
   WndClass.hInstance = hInstance;
   WndClass.hbrBackground = (HBRUSH) (COLOR_WINDOW+1);
   WndClass.hCursor = LoadCursor (NULL, IDC_ARROW);
   WndClass.hIcon = LoadIcon (NULL, IDI_APPLICATION);
   WndClass.lpszMenuName = 0;
   WndClass.lpszClassName = "WinProg";

   RegisterClass(&WndClass);

   HWND hButtonExit;
   hWindow = CreateWindow("WinProg","Window",
                     WS_OVERLAPPEDWINDOW,
                     XPos,YPos,
                     400-XPos,400-YPos,NULL,NULL,
                     hInstance, NULL);
   hButtonExit = CreateWindow("BUTTON","Exit",
```

```
                                    WS_CHILD | WS_VISIBLE |
BS_PUSHBUTTON,
                                    0,0,140,20,hWindow,(HMENU) 2,
                                    hInstance, NULL);


    ShowWindow (hWindow, nCmdShow);


    UpdateWindow (hWindow);


    SetTimer (NULL, NULL, 10, TimerProc);


    MSG Message;
    while (GetMessage(&Message, NULL, 0, 0))
    {
        DispatchMessage(&Message);
    }


    return (Message.wParam);
}


LRESULT CALLBACK WndProc (HWND hWnd, UINT uiMessage,
                          WPARAM wParam,LPARAM lParam)
{

    switch(uiMessage)
    {
        case WM_COMMAND:
            DestroyWindow (hWnd);
            return 0;
        case WM_DESTROY:
            PostQuitMessage(0);
            return 0;
        default:
            return DefWindowProc (hWnd, uiMessage,
                                  wParam, lParam);
    }
}


VOID CALLBACK TimerProc(HWND hWnd, UINT uMsg,
                        UINT idEvent, DWORD dwTime)
{
        if (XPos < 200)
```

```
{
 XPos++;
}
else
{
 XPos = 0;
}
if (YPos < 40)
{
 YPos = YPos + 4;
}
else
{
 YPos = 0;
}
SetWindowPos (hWindow, HWND_TOP, XPos,
              YPos, 400-(XPos*2), 400-(YPos*2),
              SWP_SHOWWINDOW);
}
```

12.3.2   Explanation of the source code

The `SetTimer` function is used to call a function at certain time intervals:

```
UINT SetTimer( HWND hWnd, UINT nIDEvent,
           UINT uElapse, TIMERPROC lpTimerFunc);
```

→ `hWnd` is set to NULL.
→ `nIDEvent` is set to NULL.
→ `uElapse` specifies the time interval at which the timer function is called.
→ `lpTimerFunc` is a pointer to the timer function.

The printer

13.1 General information

The printer is accessed using a device context handle in Windows. Images are drawn on the printer using the same GDI graphics commands as on the monitor. This results in substantial communication with the printer driver, which is later responsible for transmitting data to the printer. There are also other functions that signal the start of printing and the start of a new page.

13.2 An application

13.2.1 The source code

This program can access the printer using a standard Print dialog box when you click the "Print" button (see Figure 13.1 and 13.2). It then outputs the word "Printer" on the page. You must set the printer to "graphics output" beforehand.

Figure 13.1 *The application after you start it*

Figure 13.2 *The standard Print dialog box*

```
#include <windows.h>

LRESULT CALLBACK WndProc (HWND, UINT, WPARAM, LPARAM);

int APIENTRY WinMain(HINSTANCE hInstance,
                     HINSTANCE hPrevInstance,
                     LPSTR     lpCmdLine,
                     int       nCmdShow )
{
```

```
WNDCLASS WndClass;
WndClass.style = 0;
WndClass.cbClsExtra = 0;
WndClass.cbWndExtra = 0;
WndClass.lpfnWndProc = WndProc;
WndClass.hInstance = hInstance;
WndClass.hbrBackground = (HBRUSH) (COLOR_WINDOW+1);
WndClass.hCursor = LoadCursor (NULL, IDC_ARROW);
WndClass.hIcon = LoadIcon (NULL, IDI_APPLICATION);
WndClass.lpszMenuName = 0;
WndClass.lpszClassName = "WinProg";

RegisterClass(&WndClass);
HWND hWindow,hButton;
hWindow = CreateWindow("WinProg","Window",
                       WS_OVERLAPPEDWINDOW,
                       0,0,400,400,NULL,NULL,
                       hInstance, NULL);
hButton = CreateWindow("BUTTON","Print",
                       WS_CHILD | WS_VISIBLE
                       | BS_PUSHBUTTON,
                       10,340,140,20,hWindow,(HMENU) 1,
                       hInstance, NULL);

ShowWindow (hWindow, nCmdShow);

UpdateWindow (hWindow);

MSG Message;

while (GetMessage(&Message, NULL, 0, 0))
{
   DispatchMessage(&Message);
}

return (Message.wParam);
}
```

```
LRESULT CALLBACK WndProc (HWND hWnd, UINT uiMessage,
                         WPARAM wParam,LPARAM lParam)
{
   switch(uiMessage)
   {
      case WM_COMMAND:
          if (HIWORD(wParam) == BN_CLICKED)
          {
           if (LOWORD(wParam) == 1)
           {
            PRINTDLG pd;
            ZeroMemory(&pd, sizeof(PRINTDLG));
            pd.lStructSize = sizeof(PRINTDLG);
            pd.hwndOwner   = hWnd;
            pd.hDevMode    = NULL;
            pd.hDevNames   = NULL;
            pd.Flags       = PD_USEDEVMODECOPIESANDCOLLATE
                               | PD_RETURNDC;
            pd.nCopies     = 1;
            pd.nFromPage   = 0xFFFF;
            pd.nToPage     = 0xFFFF;
            pd.nMinPage    = 1;
            pd.nMaxPage    = 0xFFFF;

            if (PrintDlg(&pd) == true)
            {
             MessageBox (hWnd, "OK", "OK",MB_OK);
            }




            DOCINFO di;
            di.cbSize = sizeof(DOCINFO);
            di.lpszDocName = "Bitmap Printing Test";
            di.lpszOutput = (LPTSTR) NULL;
            di.fwType = 0;
            StartDoc(pd.hDC, &di);
            StartPage(pd.hDC);
```

```
            TextOut(pd.hDC, 10, 10, "Printer",
                    lstrlen ("Printer"));

            EndPage(pd.hDC);

            EndDoc(pd.hDC);

            DeleteDC(pd.hDC);



            }
        }
        return 0;
    case WM_DESTROY:
        PostQuitMessage(0);
        return 0;
    default:
        return DefWindowProc (hWnd, uiMessage,
                              wParam, lParam);
    }
}
```

13.2.2   Explanation of the source code

The only new features here are in the WM_COMMAND message.

Calling the standard Print dialog box

Windows provides a number of standard dialog boxes for opening files, saving
files, selecting colors, and printing. The standard Print dialog box is used in this
program. You can use this dialog box to choose the printer you want to use and
select specific settings. The dialog box also creates a device context object. You
use the PrintDlg function to create the standard Print dialog box. This function
expects a structure of the type PRINTDLG:

```
typedef struct tagPD
{
   pd DWORD lStructSize;
   HWND hwndOwner;
   HANDLE hDevMode;
```

```
    HANDLE hDevNames;
    HDC hDC;
    DWORD Flags;
    WORD nFromPage;
    WORD nToPage;
    WORD nMinPage;
    WORD nMaxPage;
    WORD nCopies;
    HINSTANCE hInstance;
    DWORD lCustData;
    LPPRINTHOOKPROC lpfnPrintHook;
    LPSETUPHOOKPROC lpfnSetupHook;
    LPCTSTR lpPrintTemplateName;
    LPCTSTR lpSetupTemplateName;
    HANDLE hPrintTemplate;
    HANDLE hSetupTemplate;
} PRINTDLG;
```

At this point we will only discuss the variables that are used. All other variables are set to NULL by `ZeroMemory`:

→ `lStructSize` is the size of the structure. It is determined using `sizeof`.

→ `HDC` is a handle to a device context object that was created by the `PrintDlg` dialog box.

→ Flags are a series of constants that are specified here. PD_RETURNDC is a flag, which indicates that a handle to the device context object for the printer is returned.

→ `nCopies` is the number of copies to be printed.

We must now use the `PrintDlg` command to call a standard dialog box. Windows provides a number of standard dialog boxes. Dialog boxes are simply windows that are used to enter data. These standard dialog boxes are called using a structure and they return values. We use the Print dialog box in this program. It is called using the `PrintDlg` command. A structure, which is used for initialization and output, is passed to this command:

```
BOOL PrintDlg( LPPRINTDLG lppd);
```

The structure described above is passed to this call in the source code:

```
PrintDlg(&pd);
```

Starting a print job

Windows provides functions that can be used to access the printer. One such function allows you to handle the printer in the same way as graphics output by simply creating a device context handle. The other functions allow you to start the print job, which then appears in the Printer Manager. The `StartDoc` function is used for this. You must then use the `StartPage` function to set up a new page. The device context is already linked to the printer driver from the time you use the `PrintDlg` function. Printing only begins, however, when the entire print job is ready. The individual functions for the printer are then called as soon as the device context has been created:

```
DOCINFO di;
            di.cbSize = sizeof(DOCINFO);
            di.lpszDocName = "Bitmap Printing Test";
            di.lpszOutput = (LPTSTR) NULL;
            di.fwType = 0;
            StartDoc(pd.hDC, &di);
            StartPage(pd.hDC);



            TextOut(pd.hDC, 10, 10, "Printer",
                    lstrlen ("Printer"));

            EndPage(pd.hDC);

            EndDoc(pd.hDC);

            DeleteDC(pd.hDC);
```

The `StartDoc` function starts a new print job:

```
int StartDoc( HDC hdc, CONST DOCINFO *lpdi);
```

➜ hdc is the handle to the device context object for which you want to create a new print job.

➜ lpdi is a pointer to a structure of the type DOCINFO. This structure is not relevant for this program. It only contains information about the names of documents and files. You only need to specify the size. The structure variable required for this is called cbSize.

The `StartPage` function starts a new page in which you can then draw using the usual GDI functions:

```
int StartPage( HDC hDC);
```

➔ hDC is the handle to the device context object for which the new page is started.

The `EndPage` function ends a page:

```
int EndPage( HDC hdc);
```

➔ hdc is the handle to the device context object.

The `EndDoc` function ends the entire print job:

```
int EndDoc( HDC hdc);
```

➔ Again, hdc is the handle to the device context object.

Once you have created a page for a print job using `StartDoc` and `StartPage`, you can draw on the page using the GDI functions. Before you use the GDI functions, however, you must normally define the dimensional unit to be used to access the device context.

Part II

Take that!

Win32 API: Data types

14.1 General information

The data types contained in the Win32 API define not only the size and type, but also how the data type is used. Many data types therefore have the same size and are numeric. This chapter lists the important data types that are defined in the Win32 API and used in the commands in this manual.

14.2 Table

Data type	Type	Use
BOOL	boolean	Return value
BYTE	8-bit unsigned integer	Standard 8-bit unsigned integer variable
COLORREF	32-bit unsigned integer	This data type is used for RGB color values. They are specified in the value using `0x00bbggrr`
DWORD	32-bit unsigned integer	Standard 32-bit unsigned integer variable
HANDLE	32-bit	General handle to an object. A segment that is activated in the memory
HBITMAP	32-bit	Handle to a Bitmap object
HBRUSH	32-bit	Handle to a Brush object
HCURSOR	32-bit	Handle to a Cursor object
HDC	32-bit	Handle to a device context, i.e. a device context object
HFILE	32-bit	HANDLE to a File object
HFONT	32-bit	Handle to a Font object
HGDIOBJ	32-bit	Specialized, general handle for GDI objects
HICON	32-bit	Handle to an Icon object
HINSTANCE	32-bit	Handle to an instance

Data type	Type	Use
HMENU	32-bit	Handle to a Menu object
HPEN	32-bit	Handle to a Pen object
HWND	32-bit	Handle to a Window object
LONG	32-bit signed integer	Standard 32-bit signed integer variable
LPARAM	32-bit	This is a parameter that is used for transferring messages
LPCSTR	Pointer of the type const char	Used for text
LPSTR	Pointer of the type char	Used for text
PVOID	Pointer to any variable type	Standard for a general pointer
TIMERPROC	Pointer to a function	Pointer to a function for the timer
UINT	32-bit unsigned	Generally used for integers
WNDPROC	Pointer to a function	Pointer to a function responsible for message processing
WORD	16-bit unsigned integer	Standard 16-bit unsigned integer variable
WPARAM	32-bit	This is a parameter that is used for transferring messages

Functions, structures, messages, and objects of the Win32 API

15

15.1 General information

This chapter describes the individual functions that have already been used in this manual and functions that have not yet been used but are very important. The relevant structures, messages and objects are also described along with these functions. All the descriptions are ordered according to the purpose for which the functions are used.

The letters I, O, R and N are used for each function parameter and return value. They indicate the most frequent usage. Pointers to data can be defined as input and output.

→ I means that the function uses this value. The value serves as *input* for the function.

→ O means that the function assigns this value. The value therefore serves as *output* for the function.

→ R means that the value is not output using the function's parameter list, but is a *return* value.

→ N is a sub-item. This value can be **NULL**. The function, which this value then has, is shown accordingly.

The header file and the library file, if necessary, as well as the support of the various 32-bit operating systems and support for ANSI and UNICODE are also specified for each function, structure and message. If this is not mentioned, only ANSI code is supported – or no support is needed because no text characters are used in the function.

And finally, a list of the supported systems is given for various functions or structures.

Support:

→ Windows NT 3.1 and higher
→ Windows 95 and higher
→ Windows CE 1.0 and higher

This list shows the operating systems under which the functions run. Programs running in Windows 95 work correctly without being recompiled, even in Windows NT, if all the functions are supported. If all the functions are also supported by Windows CE, the programs only run there if everything is recompiled because the processors are different. The existence of another processor does not mean that the principle of the Windows operating system changes – only the code of the individual functions changes, but all the functions are still available.

Other additional information:

Header file: WINUSER.H

Library file: USER32.LIB

Support for ANSI/UNICODE

Information on the function or structure is stored in the header file. This does not generally have to be integrated separately because usually it is already incorporated into the windows.h file. The library file is the file containing the compiled code. This file does not have to be supplied to the compiler because Windows fundamentals, in particular, are needed. These are incorporated automatically into Windows programs. ANSI/UNICODE determines how the text, which you want to enter in the function, must be stored. Both can be supported and the compiler selects the correct function. If only one variant is supported, you may have to use the TEXT macro to convert ANSI to UNICODE.

Win32 API: Windows fundamentals

16.1 Win32 API functions, structures, messages, and objects for Windows fundamentals

The fundamental Windows concept consists of windows. You can use them to display a number of active programs graphically. A window hierarchy was introduced for this purpose. Even the desktop window is just a window. A message concept was also developed to allow the windows to communicate with each other. You need the GDI functions to output graphics.

Functions, structures, messages, and objects	Meaning
Window object	The most important part of windowing
CreateWindow	Creates a new window
WM_CREATE	Message sent following the creation of the window object
CREATESTRUCT	Structure for the WM_CREATE message
DestroyWindow	Deletes a window object
WM_DESTROY	Message sent following the deletion of the window object
ShowWindow	Sets the display status
GetMessage	Gets messages from the message queue and waits for more messages
PeekMessage	Gets messages from the message queue and does not wait for more messages
RegisterClass	Registers a window class
WNDCLASS	Structure used by the RegisterClass function to register the window class
SetWindowText	Sets the text for a window object
TranslateMessage	Translates virtual key messages into character messages using the keyboard driver

Functions, structures, messages, and objects	Meaning
DispatchMessage	Calls the window function and passes on the message
WM_PAINT	This is sent if an area in the window is to be redrawn

Table 16.1 *Win32 API functions, structures, messages, and objects for Windows fundamentals*

16.1.1 Window object

Everything revolves around the window object in Windows. Like all other objects, the window object is a data structure for which there are certain management functions. This object contains data relating to the position, size, properties or the position in the hierarchy, among other things, and communicates only with window objects. The system and other programs, which also have window objects, control this communication. Using window objects in Windows is the only way to output graphics from a number of applications at the same time. Window objects are also the only way to get messages from the system, as well as from peripherals.

A window object is generally displayed as a standard window on the screen by the DefWindowProc function.

16.1.2 CreateWindow

The CreateWindow function creates a window object:

```
HWND CreateWindow(LPCTSTR lpClassName,
                  LPCTSTR lpWindowName,
                  DWORD dwStyle,
                  int x,
                  int y,
                  int nWidth,
                  int nHeight,
                  HWND hWndParent,
                  HMENU hMenu,
                  HANDLE hInstance,
                  LPVOID lpParam
                  );
```

→ I: lpClassName specifies the name of the window class.
→ I: lpWindowName defines the window text.

→ I: `dwStyle` determines the properties of the window. Constants can be combined by separating them using Or. The properties serve a number of purposes. For example, they define the extent of the difference in size between the window device context and the client device context. The window device context covers everything: the entire window with the title bars, menus, and so on. Window regions are also used to define which parts of the corresponding device context may actually be changed. Regions, in relation to a device context, are the areas in which text or images can be drawn. User-defined regions can also be assigned, but these are subordinate to the window regions. Window regions are therefore defined according to which area has to be redrawn, for example. These settings also define how the windows behave, when they issue messages and when something is actually redrawn.

WS_BORDER specifies that the window has a border.
WS_CAPTION defines that the window has a title bar. This constant invokes WS_BORDER.
WS_CHILD/WS_CHILDWINDOW defines that the window is a child window.
WS_CLIPCHILDREN specifies that the areas cannot be overwritten by child windows during drawing operations.
WS_CLIPSIBLINGS specifies that the areas cannot be overwritten by adjacent child windows.
WS_DISABLED defines that the window gets no further input from the system.
WS_DLGFRAME defines that the window has a frame, just like a dialog box.
WS_GROUP means that the window belongs to a group.
WS_HSCROLL specifies that the window has a horizontal scroll bar.
WS_ICONI/WS_MINIMIZE means that the window is initialized in minimized/iconized form.
WS_MAXIMIZE specifies that the window is initialized in maximized form.
WS_MAXIMIZEBOX means that the window is displayed with a Maximize button. WM_SYSMENU must also be activated.
WS_MINIMIZEBOX defines that the window is displayed with a Minimize button. WM_SYSMENU must also be activated.
WS_OVERLAPPED/WS_TILED means that the window is an overlapped window. An overlapped window is a window that can be hidden by other windows and can itself hide other windows in its area. This window has a title bar and a frame.
WS_OVERLAPPEDWINDOW/WS_TILEDWINDOW automatically implies

a number of constants. These constants are: WS_OVERLAPPED, WS_CAPTION, WS_SYSMENU, WS_THICKFRAME, WS_MINIMZEBOX and WS_MAXIMIZEBOX.

WS_POPUP defines that the window is a pop-up window. A pop-up window behaves in the same way as an overlapped window. It has no frame and no title bar, but represents only the window area.

WS_POPUPWINDOW declares that the window is made up of a number of constants. These constants are: WS_BORDER, WS_POPUP and WS_SYSMENU. WS_CAPTION must be activated in order to display a menu in the window.

WS_SIZEBOX/WS_THICKFRAME specifies that the window has a Size button.

WS_SYSMENU means that the window has a window menu in its title bar. WS_CAPTION must also be activated for this.

WS_TABSTOP specifies that the keyboard focus can be changed to this window by pressing [⇆] (tab). When you press [⇆], the keyboard focus is switched to the next window on the same level using WS_TABSTOP.

WS_VISIBLE defines that the window is initialized as visible. As a rule, all windows are initialized as invisible.

WS_VSCROLL means that the window has a vertical scroll bar.

➜ I: X and Y specify the top left position of the window. You must specify this position using screen coordinates for an independent window. In the case of a child window, this position is relative to the top left corner of the parent window. All values should be specified in pixels.
If the CW_USEDEFAULT constant is specified for the X parameter, the window is set to the default position and the value in Y is ignored.

➜ I: nWidth and nHeight specify the width and height of the window area in pixels.
If the CW_USEDEFAULT constant is specified for the nWidth parameter, the window dimensions are set to default values. The value specified in nHeight is therefore ignored.

➜ I: hWndParent specifies the handle for a parent window. A parent window is the window that is superordinate to another window. This superordinate status relates to the graphic display and to how the windows interact. The child window is the opposite to the parent window.

➜ N: If this value is NULL, the window is independent and does not have a parent window.

➜ I: hMenu is the handle to a menu object. This menu object is used to display a menu in the window. This value is used very often to specify an ID number for windows of control elements. To this end, this value must first be converted to a handle to a menu object.

→ N: If this value is NULL, the corresponding window does not contain a menu.

→ I: `hInstance` is a handle to the instance to which the window belongs. This parameter only expresses whether the window belongs to a thread. It has no effect on the object itself. You can use this parameter to specify which message queue for which thread is to be used to enter the messages containing user entries for a window.

→ I: `lpParam` specifies a value, which is added to the CREATESTRUCT structure. This structure is inserted into the message queue of the thread as a WM_CREATE message for the window object.

→ N: This parameter can be NULL. In this case, the NULL value is simply transferred as the parameter for the WM_CREATE message.

→ R/O: If the function created a window, it supplies the handle to the window object that was created as the `return value`.
If a window object was not created, the function returns the value NULL. You can use the `GetLastError` function to find out the precise meaning of the error message.

Support:

→ Windows NT 3.1 and higher
→ Windows 95 and higher
→ Windows CE 1.0 and higher

Header file: WINUSER.H

Library file: USER32.LIB

ANSI/UNICODE: Support for both in Windows NT

16.1.3   WM_CREATE

The WM _CREATE message is inserted into a message queue if a window was created for the message queue for this thread. The message is then sent to the window:

```
WM_CREATE
lpcs = (LPCREATESTRUCT) lParam;
```

→ O: `lpcs` contains a pointer to a structure of the type CREATESTRUCT. This structure contains information about the window that was created.

Support:

→ Windows NT 3.1 and higher
→ Windows 95 and higher
→ Windows CE 1.0 and higher

Header file: WINUSER.H

16.1.4 CREATESTRUCT

This structure is passed on to the WM_CREATE message. A variable of this structure is created by the CreateWindow function:

```
typedef struct tagCREATESTRUCT
{
    LPVOID lpCreateParams;
    HINSTANCE hInstance;
    HMENU hMenu;
    HWND hwndParent;
    int cy;
    int cx;
    int y;
    int x;
    LONG style;
    LPCTSTR lpszName;
    LPCTSTR lpszClass;
    DWORD dwExStyle;
} CREATESTRUCT;
```

→ O: lpCreateParams contains the parameter that was specified in the CreateWindow function.
→ O: hInstance contains the handle to the thread to which the window belongs.
→ O: hMenu contains the handle to the menu object that was specified for the window.
→ O: hWndParent contains the handle to the window object that was specified as the higher-level or parent window for the window.
→ O: cy, cx, y and x contain values relating to the position and size of the window. These values can appear as relative or absolute values in relation to the screen.
→ O: style contains the properties of the window.
→ O: lpszName contains the name of the window.
→ O: lpszClass contains the name of the window class on which the window is based.
→ O: dwExStyle reflects the properties of the window, as defined by the CreateWindowEx function. These are the WS_EX styles.

Support:

→ Windows NT 3.1 and higher
→ Windows 95 and higher
→ Windows CE 1.0 and higher

Header file: WINUSER.H

Always available as ANSI/UNICODE

16.1.5   DestroyWindow

The DestroyWindow function deletes a window object. Before this happens, the WM_DESTROY and WM_NCDESTROY messages are inserted into the queue for the thread to which the window belongs. This is done in order to deactivate the window and lose its input focus. This function also deletes the menu in the window, cleans up the queue for the thread, deletes the timer, and releases the clipboard:

```
BOOL DestroyWindow( HWND hWnd);
```

→ I: hwnd is the handle to the window object to be deleted.
→ O/R: If the function deleted the window object, the return value is not NULL.

If the window object was not deleted or if another error occurred, the return value is NULL. You can get more information about the error using the GetLastError function.

Support:

→ Windows NT 3.1 and higher
→ Windows 95 and higher
→ Windows CE 1.0 and higher

Header file: WINUSER.H

Library file: USER32.LIB

16.1.6   WM_DESTROY

The DestroyWindow function sends the WM_DESTROY message to the window that you want to delete. WM_DESTROY is sent before the window object is deleted:

```
WM_DESTROY
```

This message has no parameters.

Support:

→ Windows NT 3.1 and higher
→ Windows 95 and higher
→ Windows CE 1.0 and higher

Header file: WINUSER.H

16.1.7   ShowWindow

The ShowWindow function determines how the window is displayed. The window object is modified for this purpose. The values of this function are evaluated by the GetDC function, for example.

```
BOOL ShowWindow (HWND hWnd, int nCmdShow);
```

→ I: hWnd is the handle to the window whose display properties are to be changed.
→ I: nCmdShow determines which value is set for the display status in the window object. One of the following constants defines how the window is displayed.

SW_SHOW activates the window and displays it with the current settings.
SW_HIDE hides the window and activates another window.
SW_MAXIMIZE maximizes the window.
SW_MINIMIZE minimizes the window. The next window in the hierarchy is then activated.
SW_RESTORE has almost the same effect as SW_SHOW. You should use this constant if you want to restore a minimized window.
SW_SHOWDEFAULT specifies that the display is set using data that was transferred to the application when you started it. An application is normally started using the CreateProcess function. The display value is transferred there in the STARTUP structure.
SW_SHOWMAXIMIZED defines that the window is activated and maximized.
SW_SHOWMINIMIZED specifies that the window is activated and minimized.
SW_SHOWMINNOACTIVE specifies that the active window remains activated and is minimized.
SW_SHOWNA/SW_SHOWNOACTIVE declares that the active window remains activated and that it uses the current data for display.
SW_SHOWNORMAL activates the window and displays it with the current data.

→ O/R: If the window was visible beforehand, the function returns a value other than NULL.

→ N: If the window was invisible beforehand, the function returns the value NULL.

Support:

→ Windows NT 3.1 and higher
→ Windows 95 and higher
→ Windows CE 1.0 and higher

Header file: WINUSER.H

Library file: USER32.LIB

16.1.8   GetMessage

The `GetMessage` function obtains the messages for a given window and its child windows from the message queue. Only the messages for the windows of the calling thread are processed, however. Messages from other windows cannot be processed. This function, along with other functions, normally forms the core component of Windows programs. It is used in connection with a While loop to perform message processing. The program is then closed by the WM_QUIT message. If the message queue does not contain any messages, the `GetMessage` function makes sure that the program does not get any more processor time until a new message arrives in the message queue. This is the main difference between this function and the `PeekMessage` function.

```
BOOL GetMessage( LPMSG lpMsg, HWND hWnd,
                 UINT wMsgFilterMin, UINT wMsgFilterMax);
```

→ O: `lpMsg` is a pointer to a MSG structure. This structure contains information about the type of message.
→ I: `hWnd` is the handle to a window of the calling thread from which the messages are to be retrieved.
→ N: If this parameter is NULL, the function picks out all the messages for all the windows of the calling thread.
→ I: `wMsgFilterMin` specifies the lowest range of the messages.
→ N: If the specified value is NULL, there is no lower limit.
→ I: `wMsgFilterMax` defines the highest range of the messages.
→ N: If the specified value is NULL, there is no upper limit.

➔ O/R: If the function picks out a message other than WM_QUIT, it returns a value other than NULL.

If the function picks out the WM_QUIT message, it returns the value NULL.

If an error occurs while executing the function, the function returns the value –1. You can get more information about the error using the Get-LastError function.

Support:

➔ Windows NT 3.1 and higher
➔ Windows 95 and higher
➔ Windows CE 1.0 and higher

Header file: WINUSER.H

Library file: USER32.LIB

Always available as ANSI/UNICODE in Windows NT.

16.1.9   PeekMessage

The PeekMessage function processes messages from the message queue. The function can remove the messages from the message queue or leave them there. It does not ensure that the thread does not get any more processor time, but the thread is executed in the usual way. This is the main difference between this function and GetMessage. This function should be called when you need to process messages from the queue in a possibly non-destructive way. Applications such as simple games often use this function. Messages are only selected for windows of the calling thread. You can specify the window whose messages you want to process. The function also picks out all the messages for the child windows as well:

```
BOOL PeekMessage(LPMSG lpMsg, HWND hWnd,
                 UINT wMsgFilterMin, UINT wMsgFilterMax,
                 UINT wRemoveMsg);
```

➔ O: lpMsg is a pointer to a MSG structure. This structure contains data relating to the message type.
➔ I: hWnd is the handle to the window object for which you want the function to pick out messages.
➔ N: If the value is NULL, the function picks all the messages for the calling thread from the message queue.
➔ I: wMsgFilterMin specifies the lower value range of the messages.
➔ N: If this value is NULL, there is no lower value range.

➡️ I: `wMsgFilterMax` specifies the upper value range of the messages.

➡️ N: If this value is NULL, there is no upper value range.

➡️ `wRemoveMsg` is a value that is specified by constants. This value determines whether the messages are to be removed from the queue or whether they should remain there. Only one of the following constants can be specified for this. You also have the option of using other constants, which specify whether a specific type of message is to be retrieved from the message queue.

PM_NOREMOVE specifies that the messages remain in the message queue.
PM_REMOVE establishes that the messages do not remain in the message queue.

Normally, all the messages are picked out of the message queue. This selection is only influenced by `hWnd`. You can speed up the selection by specifying one of the following constants. One or more of these constants can also be specified in addition to the constants mentioned above.

You can use these constants only in Windows 98 and Windows NT 5.0.
PM_QS_INPUT specifies that messages triggered using the mouse are to be selected from the message queue under messages triggered by the keyboard.
PM_QS_PAINT instructs the function to pick out PAINT messages.
PM_QS_POSTMESSAGE instructs the function to pick out all the messages that were written to the queue using `PostMessage`. In addition, all timer and hot key messages are read out.
PM_QS_SENDMESSAGE instructs the function to pick out all the messages from the message queue that were sent to the message queue using the `SendMessage` function.

➡️ O/R: If a message was removed, the function returns a value that is not equal to NULL.

➡️ N: If the function did not find a message, it supplies the value NULL as the `return value`.

Support:

➡️ Windows NT 3.1 and higher
➡️ Windows 95 and higher
➡️ Windows CE 1.0 and higher

Header file: WINUSER.H

Library file: USER32.LIB

Always available as ANSI/UNICODE in Windows NT.

16.1.10   RegisterClass

The RegisterClass function registers a window class. This window class can be used later by CreateWindow. A window class is a data structure that sets property data and assigns a message handling function to the window object at the start:

```
ATOM RegisterClass (CONST WNDCLASS *lpWndClass);
```

➔ I: lpWndClass is a pointer to a structure of the type WNDCLASS. This structure contains the data for the window class.
➔ O/R: An ATOM (an integer value that points to a string in a list, an atom table) is supplied as the return value. The string identifies the class.
➔ N: If an error occurs, the function returns the value NULL. You can get more information about the error using the GetLastError function.

Support:

➔ Windows NT 3.1 and higher
➔ Windows 95 and higher
➔ Windows CE 1.0 and higher

Header file: WINUSER.H

Library file: USER32.LIB

Always available as ANSI/UNICODE in Windows NT.

16.1.11   WNDCLASS

The WNDCLASS structure contains all the data that is supplied to a window class:

```
typedef struct _WNDCLASS
{
    UINT    style;
    WNDPROC lpfnWndProc;
    int     cbClsExtra;
    int     cbWndExtra;
    HANDLE  hInstance;
    HICON   hIcon;
    HCURSOR hCursor;
    HBRUSH  hbrBackground;
    LPCTSTR lpszMenuName;
```

```
   LPCTSTR lpszClassName;
} WNDCLASS;
```

→ I: `style` specifies the class properties and basic properties of the window. These include the `CreateWindow` properties. The basic properties can consist of a combination of the constants listed below. The class properties, on the other hand, are not only the basic properties of the window, but they also determine the properties of the class, e.g. whether the class may also be used by other threads to create windows.

CS_CLASSDC specifies that a device context is used by all the windows in the class.

CS_DBLCLKS means that a message is sent by double-clicking the window if the cursor is in this window.

CS_GLOBALCLASS establishes that the value of `hInstance` is not important for the class. If this constant is not activated, a window can only be created using the same `hInstance` value as is defined for the class.

CS_HREDRAW specifies that the entire window is to be redrawn if the position or size specified for the width of the client area of the window is changed.

CS_VREDRAW defines that the entire window is to be redrawn if the position or size specified for the height of the client area of the window is changed.

CS_NOCLOSE specifies that you can no longer select "Close" in the window menu.

CS_OWNDC instructs the function to create a separate device context for each window.

CS_PARENTDC establishes that the clipping region of the child window is set to the size of the parent window.

CS_SAVEBITS defines that a window saves the pixels that it covers. The window uses this data to restore the graphics in the event of the window being moved. This only happens when no changes were made to the underlying graphics area in the interim period. The advantage of this procedure is that fewer WM_PAINT messages are sent.

CS_BYTEALIGNCLIENT specifies that the client area of a window is defined from the position on the screen by the byte limit in a horizontal direction.

CS_BYTEALIGNWINDOW means that a window is defined from the position on the screen by the byte limit in a horizontal direction.

16

TAKE THAT!

→ I: `lpfnWndProc` is a pointer to a function. This function is the one used to process messages for this window. This function, in turn, is called by the `DispatchMessage` function.

→ I: `cbClsExtra` defines the number of extra bytes that follow the class structure when it is registered. These bytes are set to NULL.

→ I: `cbWndExtra` specifies the number of extra bytes that follow the window object that was created. You can set these bytes using `SetWindowLong` after you have created the window.

→ I: `hInstance` is the handle to the instance containing the function for the window class.

→ I: `hIcon` specifies the handle to an icon, where this icon is a resource. Resources can also be created from files during runtime. They do not necessarily have to exist in the application file.

→ N: If the value is NULL, the window has a standard icon.

→ I: `hCursor` specifies the handle to a cursor.

→ N: If this value is NULL, the window does not have a special cursor; the window's cursor is the cursor that was previously set.

→ I: `hbrBackground` specifies the handle to a Brush object. This Brush object is used by default to redraw the window's background using `BeginPaint`. There is a whole range of predefined system Brush objects. These objects define all the colors, but there are only twenty system colors. You can designate these system colors under Display in the control panel.

COLOR_ACTIVEBORDER
COLOR_ACTIVECAPTION
COLOR_APPWORKSPACE
COLOR_BACKGROUND
COLOR_BTNFACE
COLOR_BTNSHADOW
COLOR_BTNTEXT
COLOR_CAPTIONTEXT
COLOR_GRAYTEXT
COLOR_HIGHLIGHT
COLOR_HIGHLIGHTTEXT
COLOR_INACTIVEBORDER
COLOR_INACTIVECAPTION
COLOR_MENU
COLOR_MENUTEXT
COLOR_SCROLLBAR
COLOR_WINDOW
COLOR_WINDOWFRAME

COLOR_WINDOWTEXT

→ N: If this value is set to NULL, the window's background is not redrawn.
→ I: `lpszMenuName` specifies the resource name for a menu.
→ N: If this value is NULL, the window does not have a menu. Every window must then be assigned its own menu.
→ I: `lpszClassName` specifies the name of the window class. However, this parameter can also be an ATOM, which must have been created beforehand using AddGobalAtom. This is simply another reference to the name.

Support:

→ Windows NT 3.1 and higher
→ Windows 95 and higher
→ Windows CE 1.0 and higher

Header file: WINUSER.H

Always available as ANSI/UNICODE.

16.1.12 TranslateMessage

The `TranslateMessage` function translates messages containing virtual key codes into messages containing character codes. The keyboard driver is used to create a virtual key code from the scan codes, depending on the country setting. This virtual key code is added to the message queue as a message. The `TranslateMessage` function creates ANSI codes from these virtual key codes, depending on the country setting. These ANSI codes are then added to the message queue again in the form of a new message.

```
BOOL TranslateMessage( CONST MSG *lpMsg);
```

→ I: `lpMsg` is a pointer to a MSG structure. This MSG structure is checked for messages that can be converted. This function is generally used in the middle of the While loop so that it can check every message.
→ O/R: If the message was translated, the return value is not NULL.
→ N: If the message was not translated, the return value is NULL.

Support:

→ Windows NT 3.1 and higher
→ Windows 95 and higher
→ Windows CE 1.0 and higher

Header file: WINUSER.H

Library file: USER32.LIB

16.1.13 DispatchMessage

The `DispatchMessage` function calls the window function. It then passes the message on to this function:

```
LONG DispatchMessage( CONST MSG *lpmsg);
```

→ I: `lpmsg` is a pointer to a MSG structure. This MSG structure contains the message that is sent to the window function to which the message is addressed.

→ O/R: The `return value` from this function is the value, which the messages also supply as the `return value`.

Support:

→ Windows NT 3.1 and higher
→ Windows 95 and higher
→ Windows CE 1.0 and higher

Header file: WINUSER.H

Library file: USER32.LIB

Always available as ANSI/UNICODE in Windows NT.

16.1.14 WM_PAINT

The WM_PAINT message is sent when an area of the window needs to be redrawn. The message is passed to the device context of the client area of the window. The WM_NCPAINT message controls how the border and title bar are redrawn. This is performed by the `DefWindowProc` function. The WM_PAINT message is normally processed in isolation of other messages. Naturally, the region of the device context is restricted to the area to be redrawn. In connection with the WM_PAINT message, you also use the `BeginPaint` and `EndPaint` functions, which declare the areas to be redrawn as valid again.

```
WM_PAINT
hdc = (HDC) wParam;
```

→ hdc is the device context of the client area of the window in which a certain area is to be redrawn. The area is specified by a region, which was set with a higher priority.

Support:

→ Windows NT 3.1 and higher
→ Windows 95 and higher
→ Windows CE 1.0 and higher

Header file: WINUSER.H

16.2 Examples

16.2.1 Creating a normal window

We want to create a normal, overlapped window (see Figure 16.1).

Figure 16.1 *The application after you start it*

The source code

```c
#include <windows.h>

LRESULT CALLBACK WndProc (HWND, UINT, WPARAM, LPARAM);

int APIENTRY WinMain(HINSTANCE hInstance,
                     HINSTANCE hPrevInstance,
                     LPSTR     lpCmdLine,
                     int       nCmdShow )
{
   WNDCLASS WndClass;
   WndClass.style = 0;
   WndClass.cbClsExtra = 0;
   WndClass.cbWndExtra = 0;
   WndClass.lpfnWndProc = WndProc;
   WndClass.hInstance = hInstance;
   WndClass.hbrBackground = (HBRUSH) (COLOR_WINDOW+1);
   WndClass.hCursor = LoadCursor (NULL, IDC_ARROW);
   WndClass.hIcon = LoadIcon (NULL, IDI_APPLICATION);
   WndClass.lpszMenuName = 0;
   WndClass.lpszClassName = "WinProg";

   RegisterClass(&WndClass);

   HWND hWindow;
   hWindow = CreateWindow("WinProg","Window",
                     WS_OVERLAPPEDWINDOW,
                     0,0,600,460,NULL,NULL,
                     hInstance, NULL);

   ShowWindow (hWindow, nCmdShow);

   UpdateWindow (hWindow);


   MSG Message;
   while (GetMessage(&Message, NULL, 0, 0))
   {
      DispatchMessage(&Message);
   }

   return (Message.wParam);
```

```
}


LRESULT CALLBACK WndProc (HWND hWnd, UINT uiMessage,
                          WPARAM wParam,LPARAM lParam)
{
   switch(uiMessage)
   {
      case WM_DESTROY:
         PostQuitMessage(0);
         return 0;
      default:
         return DefWindowProc (hWnd, uiMessage,
                               wParam, lParam);
   }
}
```

Win32 API: GDI

17.1 Win32 API functions, structures, messages, and objects for the GDI

The GDI (*Graphics Device Interface*) is an interface for graphics devices. It provides functions that provide an interface to the graphics device. These functions then call driver functions. The drivers, in turn, must provide the functions that are called from the GDI.

The GDI functions allow you to communicate with the computer's graphics hardware without having to access the hardware directly. This task is performed jointly by the GDI and the drivers. The graphic output generated can be used for both the graphics card and printer output. Both devices can only be accessed independently through the GDI API, however, because the drivers allow the devices to appear identical.

You can use GDI functions to get device contexts, or rather device context objects. These device context objects can only refer to sub-areas of the device and its output. Only in these device contexts can you use graphics functions. We use the word "device context" here to refer to a device context object, which describes the area of a device and its output. Device contexts can contain two types of *regions*, those that are visible and will be used to display the output from a graphic function and those which are hidden and used to hold updates before they are displayed. The GDI provides the connection to the graphics hardware and allows you to generate graphics. It is a fundamental part of the Win32 API.

The GDI is necessary in order to implement the graphic output of the window concept. You can determine a device context from any window. The regions of the device context are designed in such a way that drawing only occurs where there are areas that have to be recreated. One window tells another that an area of a window has to be redrawn. This can be the case, for example, when windows are moved and one window leaves part of another window free.

Functions, structures, messages, and objects	Meaning
Device context object	A device context object is the object with which the GDI is mainly concerned
BeginPaint	The BeginPaint function makes all the areas valid again and returns a handle to a device context object that specifies the parts of the client area of a window that are to be redrawn
EndPaint	Draws a device context at the end of a drawing operation that was started by BeginPaint
PAINTSTRUCT	The structure of the type PAINTSTRUCT contains drawing information from BeginPaint
GetDC	Returns a handle to a device context object that specifies the entire client area of a window. This area must not be overlapped
ReleaseDC	Indicates the end of a drawing operation that was started by GetDC or GetWindowDC
GetWindowDC	Returns a handle to a device context that specifies the entire area of a window. This area must not be overlapped by other windows
SetPixel	The SetPixel function sets a pixel in a device context to a certain color
GetPixel	The GetPixel function returns the color value of a pixel
MoveToEx	Sets the drawing point in a device context to a certain position
POINT	Specifies the position of a point
LineTo	The LineTo function draws a line from the drawing point that was set to a specified point using the Pen object that was set
PolyLine	The PolyLine function draws a series of lines that are linked to the Pen object

Functions, structures, messages, and objects	Meaning
PolyBezier	The PolyBezier function draws a Bezier curve using the Pen object
Rectangle	The Rectangle function draws a box. The Pen object is used for the border color and the Brush object is used for the background color
FillRect	The FillRect function draws a filled box using the Brush object
RECT	The RECT structure describes the points of a box
Ellipse	The Ellipse function draws an ellipse. The border is drawn using the Pen object and the background is drawn using the Brush object
CreatePen	The CreatePen function creates a Pen object
Pen object	The Pen object is an object that is linked to a device context and generally determines the border color for a drawing function
SelectObject	The SelectObject function connects a device context to a certain GDI object, such as a Pen object, a Brush object or a Region object
DeleteObject	The DeleteObject function deletes a certain GDI object, such as a Pen object, a Brush object or a Region object
CreateSolidBrush	The CreateSolidBrush function creates a Brush object with a certain color
Brush object	The Brush object is an object that is linked to a device context and defines the background color for a drawing function
TextOut	The TextOut function writes a string to a certain place
SetTextColor	The SetTextColor function sets the text color of a device context
SetBkColor	The SetBkColor function sets the background color of a device context. This function is also used to set the background for TextOut
SetTextAlign	The SetTextAlign function specifies the text alignment for a device context
SetBkMode	The SetBkMode function specifies an additional property for the background color

Functions, structures, messages, and objects	Meaning
RGB	The RGB macro makes one color from color components
CreateRectRgn	The CreateRectRgn function creates a Region object shaped like a rectangle or box
Region object	The Region object is an object that specifies a device context for a specific area in which drawing is permitted
CombineRgn	The CombineRegion function combines regions in various ways
SetWindowRgn	The SetWindowRgn function assigns a region to a specific window. This region is then passed on to the device context, which is determined from this window
GetWindowRgn	The GetWindowRgn function determines the region of a window
GetStockObject	The GetStockObject function supplies a handle to a predefined object
DrawText	The DrawText function displays text on the screen

Table 17.1 *Win32 API functions, structures, messages, and objects for the GDI*

17.1.1 Device context object

The device context object is the most important object of the GDI. Practically all the other objects are linked to it. The device context object is the object in which text and graphics can be drawn using GDI functions. It describes a memory area of the graphic output device. The areas, in which the drawings take effect, are assigned to the object using regions.

17.1.2 BeginPaint

The BeginPaint functions sets the clipping region of a device context, to exclude any area outside the desired update region. This means that there are no areas that have to be redrawn. As a result, no more WM_PAINT messages are triggered. The region of the device context is therefore reduced further. This is why this function is mainly used in connection with the WM_PAINT message. This function also returns a handle to a device context object, if one exists. If the window is not displayed, it is obvious that one does not exist. The function also supplies information about the area, which it has already drawn, in a PAINTSTRUCT structure. The function redraws the areas using the Brush object specified in the `WNDCLASS` structure. This ensures that no graphics errors are made in the `WM_PAINT` message.

```
HDC BeginPaint( HWND hwnd, LPPAINTSTRUCT lpPaint);
```

→ I: hwnd is the handle to the window object from which the device context handle is to be determined.
→ I: lpPaint is a pointer to a structure of the type PAINTSTRUCT. This structure contains additional drawing information.
→ O/R: The handle to a device context of the client area is supplied as the return value. This only specifies the region that is to be redrawn.
→ N: If there is no device context available for the window because it is not currently displayed, the function returns the value NULL. You can get more information on errors in Windows NT using the GetLastError function.

Support:

→ Windows NT 3.1 and higher
→ Windows 95 and higher
→ Windows CE 1.0 and higher

Header file: WINUSER.H

Library file: USER32.LIB

17.1.3 EndPaint

The EndPaint function identifies the end of a drawing operation in a device context object; you must call this function after BeginPaint:

```
BOOL EndPaint( HWND hWnd, CONST PAINTSTRUCT *lpPaint);
```

→ I: hWnd is the handle to the window whose device context you want to access.
→ I: lpPaint is a pointer to the structure of the type PAINTSTRUCT, which is returned by the BeginPaint function.
→ O/R: A value other than NULL is always supplied as the return value.

Support:

→ Windows NT 3.1 and higher
→ Windows 95 and higher
→ Windows CE 1.0 and higher

Header file: WINUSER.H

Library file: USER32.LIB

17.1.4   PAINTSTRUCT

The structure of the type PAINTSTRUCT contains drawing information, which is supplied by the BeginPaint function:

```
typedef struct tagPAINTSTRUCT
{
    HDC   hdc;
    BOOL  fErase;
    RECT  rcPaint;
    BOOL  fRestore;
    BOOL  fIncUpdate;
    BYTE  rgbReserved[32];
} PAINTSTRUCT;
```

→ O: hdc contains the handle to a device context in which you intend to draw.

→ O: fErase determines whether the background has to be redrawn or whether this was already done by BeginPaint. The background must be redrawn if no Brush object was specified in the window class.

→ rcPaint is a structure of the type RECT, which specifies a rectangular area to be redrawn.

→ fRestore is reserved because fRestore is used internally.

→ fIncUpdate is reserved because fIncUpdate is used internally.

→ rgbReserved[32] is reserved because rgbReserved[32] is used internally.

Support:

→ Windows NT 3.1 and higher
→ Windows 95 and higher
→ Windows CE 1.0 and higher

Header file: WINUSER.H

17.1.5   GetDC

The GetDC function returns a device context for the entire client area of a window or the entire screen. This area must not be overlapped by other windows. Unlike BeginPaint, this function actually supplies a handle to an object that specifies the entire client area that is available:

```
HDC GetDC( HWND hWnd);
```

→ I: hWnd specifies the handle of the window whose client area is to be returned.
N: If this value is NULL, the function returns a device context for the entire screen. This is only possible in Windows 98, Windows NT 5.0 or later versions.

→ O/R: The handle to a device context is supplied as the return value.

→ N: If there is no device context for the window because the window is not displayed, the value NULL is returned. You can find out more about errors in Windows NT using the GetLastError function.

Support:

→ Windows NT 3.1 and higher
→ Windows 95 and higher
→ Windows CE 1.0 and higher

Header file: WINUSER.H

Library file: USER32.LIB

17.1.6   ReleaseDC

The ReleaseDC function indicates the end of a drawing operation that was started by the GetDC or GetWindowDC function:

```
int ReleaseDC( HWND hWnd, HDC hDC);
```

→ I: hWnd is the handle to a window object whose device context is to be released.

→ I: hDC is the handle to the device context of the window that was specified by hWnd.

→ O/R: If the device context was released, the function returns the value 1.

→ N: If the device context was not released, the function returns the value NULL. You can find out more about errors in Windows NT using the GetLastError function.

Support:

→ Windows NT 3.1 and higher
→ Windows 95 and higher
→ Windows CE 1.0 and higher

Header file: WINUSER.H

Library file: USER32.LIB

17.1.7 GetWindowDC

The GetWindowDC function returns a handle to a device context object that refers to the entire area, not just the client area, of the window. This area must not be overlapped:

```
HDC GetWindowDC( HWND hWnd);
```

→ I: hWnd is the handle to a window whose device context is to be determined. This device context refers to the entire window, not just the client sub-area.

→ N: If this value is NULL, the GetWindowDC function returns a device context for the entire screen without restrictions. This function can only be used in Windows 98, Windows NT 5.0 or later versions.

→ O/R: The GetWindowDC function supplies a handle to a device context that refers to the entire window as the return value.

→ N: If an error occurs, the function returns the value NULL. You can get more information on errors in Windows NT using the GetLastError function.

Support:

→ Windows NT 3.1 and higher
→ Windows 95 and higher
→ Windows CE 1.0 and higher

Header file: WINUSER.H

Library file: USER32.LIB

17.1.8 SetPixel

The SetPixel function sets a pixel of a device context to a specific color value. If this is not available, the function determines the value that is most similar to the desired color value:

```
COLORREF SetPixel(HDC hdc, int X, int Y,
                  COLORREF crColor);
```

→ hdc is the handle to the device context object in which you want to redraw.

→ X, Y are relative, logical values that refer to the top left corner of the device context.

→ crColor is the color value to which the pixel is to be set.

→ O/R: If the function sets the pixel to a color value, it returns this color value. This can be different from the desired color value because it may be changed this color cannot be displayed.

→ N: If an error occurs, the function returns the value −1. You can get more information on errors in Windows NT using the `GetLastError` function.

Support:

→ Windows NT 3.1 and higher
→ Windows 95 and higher
→ Windows CE 1.0 and higher

Header file: WINGDI.H

Library file: GDI32.LIB

17.1.9 GetPixel

The `GetPixel` function returns the color value of a pixel of a device context; its position is also specified:

```
COLORREF GetPixel( HDC hdc, int XPos, int nYPos);
```

→ hdc is the handle to a device context object for which you want to determine the color value of a pixel.

→ XPos and YPos specify the position relative to the top left corner of the device context object.

→ O/R: The color value of the pixel at the corresponding position is supplied as the `return value`. If the desired color value is not within the region from which you can determine color values, the value of a constant is returned.

Support:

→ Windows NT 3.1 and higher
→ Windows 95 and higher
→ Windows CE 1.0 and higher

Header file: WINGDI.H

Library file: GDI32.LIB

17.1.10 MoveToEx

The `MoveToEx` function sets the drawing point. Every device context has a drawing point. This is specified relative to the top left corner of the device context. You can establish the value of this drawing point using the `MoveToEx` function.

The relative X and Y coordinates are specified at the same time. The position is then used by drawing functions:

```
BOOL MoveToEx( HDC hdc, int X, int Y, LPPOINT lpPOINT);
```

→ I: hdc is the handle to a device context. The drawing point is set in this device context.

→ I: X and Y are the relative, logical positions from the top left corner of the device context. These determine the drawing point.

→ O: lpPOINT is a pointer to a structure. Data relating to the position of the drawing point is returned in this structure.

→ O/R: If the function is executed without errors, the function returns a value other than NULL.

→ N: If an error occurs while executing the function, the function returns the value NULL. You can find out more about the error in Windows NT using the GetLastError function.

Support:

→ Windows NT 3.1 and higher
→ Windows 95 and higher
→ Windows CE not supported

Header file: WINGDI.H

Library file: GDI32.LIB

17.1.11 POINT

The POINT structure defines the location of a point. This point is described by logical X and Y values:

```
typedef struct tagPOINT
{
    LONG x;
    LONG y;
} POINT;
```

→ I/O: X and Y are position specifications. These specifications are logical values, which you can use to describe a point logically from a top left corner.

Support:

→ Windows NT 3.1 and higher
→ Windows 95 and higher
→ Windows CE 1.0 and higher

Header file: WINDEF.H

17.1.12 LineTo

The `LineTo` function draws a line from the specified drawing point to a specific point using `MoveToEx`. `LineTo` uses the settings for the Pen object to give its line a color and other properties:

```
BOOL LineTo( HDC hdc, int nXEnd, int nYEnd);
```

> → I: hdc is the handle to the device context in which the line is to be drawn.
> → I: nXEnd and nYEnd are specifications for a point relative to the top left corner of the device context to which the line is drawn. The line starts at the point specified by MoveToEx.
> → O/R: If the function is executed without errors, the function returns a value other than NULL.
> → N: If an error occurs while executing the function, however, the function returns the value NULL. You can find out more information about the error using the GetLastError function in Windows NT.

Support:

> → Windows NT 3.1 and higher
> → Windows 95 and higher
> → Windows CE not supported

Header file: WINGDI.H

Library file: GDI32.LIB

17.1.13 PolyLine

The `PolyLine` function draws a series of connected lines to create a polygon. The points of the lines are specified by an array of the type `POINT`:

```
BOOL PolyLine( HDC hdc, CONST POINT *lppt, int cPOINTs);
```

> → I: hdc is the handle to a device context in which the lines are to be drawn.
> → I: lppt is the pointer to an array of POINT structures that are used for input. The input consists of the points that make up the lines. The number of points must be at least two.
> → I: cPOINTs specifies the number of points in the structure to which lppt points.

17

→ O/R: If the function is executed without errors, the function returns a value other than NULL.

→ N: If an error occurs while executing the function, the function returns the value NULL. To find out more about the error, you must call the Get-LastError function. This only works in Windows NT, however.

Support:

→ Windows NT 3.1 and higher
→ Windows 95 and higher
→ Windows CE 1.0 and higher

Header file: WINGDI.H

Library file: GDI32.LIB

17.1.14 PolyBezier

The PolyBezier function draws a sequence of lines using Bezier curves:

```
BOOL PolyBezier( HDC hdc, CONST POINT *lppt,
                 DWORD cPOINTs);
```

→ I: hdc is the handle to a device context in which the sequence of lines is to be drawn.
→ I: lppt is a pointer to a series of POINT structures. These structures specify the points between the Bezier lines.
→ I: cPOINTs specifies the number of points.
→ O/R: If the function is executed without errors, the function returns a value other than NULL.
→ N: If an error occurs while executing the function, the function returns the value NULL. To find out more about the error, you must call the Get-LastError function. This only works in Windows NT, however.

Support:

→ Windows NT 3.1 and higher
→ Windows 95 and higher
→ Windows CE not supported

Header file: WINGDI.H

Library file: GDI32.LIB

17.1.15 Rectangle

The `Rectangle` function draws a box or rectangle. It uses the Pen object for the border color and the Brush object for the background color:

```
BOOL Rectangle( HDC hdc, int nLeftRect, int nTopRect,
                int nRightRect, int nBottomRect);
```

→ I: hdc is a handle to a device context object in which the box is to be drawn.
→ I: nLeftRect, nTopRect, nRightRect and nBottomRect specify a relative, logical position for the box.
→ O/R: If the function is executed without errors, the function returns a value other than NULL.
→ N: If an error occurs while executing the function, the function returns the value NULL. To find out more about the error, you must call the Get-LastError function. This only works in Windows NT, however.

Support:

→ Windows NT 3.1 and higher
→ Windows 95 and higher
→ Windows CE 1.0 and higher

Header file: WINGDI.H

Library file: GDI32.LIB

17.1.16 FillRect

The `FillRect` function draws a filled box or rectangle. To do this, the function uses the Brush object that was set:

```
int FillRect( HDC hDC, CONST RECT *lprc, HBRUSH hbr);
```

→ I: hdc is the handle to a device context in which the filled box is drawn. A special feature of this function is that the top left corner includes the edge, while the bottom right corner excludes the edge.
→ I: lprc is a pointer to a RECT structure. This RECT structure contains specifications relating to the position and size of the box.
→ I: hbr is the Brush object that is used to draw the box.
→ O/R: If the function is executed without errors, the function returns a value other than NULL.
→ N: If an error occurs while executing the function, the function returns the value NULL. To find out more about the error, you must call the Get-LastError function. This only works in Windows NT, however.

Support:

- → Windows NT 3.1 and higher
- → Windows 95 and higher
- → Windows CE 1.0 and higher

Header file: WINUSER.H

Library file: USER32.LIB

17.1.17 RECT

The RECT structure describes the specifications for a rectangle or box. Two points are described using coordinates, where the box then extends between these two points:

```
typedef struct _RECT
{
   LONG left;
   LONG top;
   LONG right;
   LONG bottom;
} RECT;
```

- → I/O: left, top, right and bottom specify two points. The box is then drawn between these two points.

Support:

- → Windows NT 3.1 and higher
- → Windows 95 and higher
- → Windows CE 1.0 and higher

Header file: WINDEF.H

17.1.18 Ellipse

The Ellipse function draws an ellipse. The Pen object that was set is used to draw the border of the ellipse, while the current Brush object is used to fill its background:

```
BOOL Ellipse( HDC hdc, int nLeftRect, int nTopRect,
              int nRightRect, int nBottomRect);
```

- → hdc is the handle to the device context in which the ellipse is drawn.

→ nLeftRect, nTopRect, nRightRect, nBottomRect are the specifications for two points, which show the extent of a box. The ellipse is drawn in this box.

→ O/R: If the function is executed without errors, the function returns a value other than NULL .

→ N: If an error occurs while executing the function, the function returns the value NULL. To find out more about the error, you must call the Get-LastError function. This only works in Windows NT, however.

Support:

→ Windows NT 3.1 and higher
→ Windows 95 and higher
→ Windows CE 1.0 and higher

Header file: WINGDI.H

Library file: GDI32.LIB

17.1.19   CreatePen

The CreatePen function creates a Pen object. The Pen object is generally used to draw the border in certain drawing functions. To this end, the Pen object is linked to the device context using the SelectObject function:

```
HPEN CreatePen( int fnPenStyle, int nWidth,
                COLORREF crColor);
```

→ I: fnPenStyle is determined by a constant. The constants can only be used individually.

PS_SOLID creates a normal Pen object, which is used to draw solid lines.
PS_DASH creates a Pen object, which draws dashes instead of a solid line. This is only possible if nWidth is one or less than one.
PS_DOT creates a Pen object, which draws dotted lines. This is only possible if nWidth is one or less than one.
PS_DASHDOT specifies that the line that is drawn consists of dashes and dots. This is only possible if nWidth is one or less than one.
PS_DASHDOTDOT means that the line that is drawn consists of the following recurring sequence: dash, dot and dot. This is only possible if nWidth is one or less than one.
PS_NULL specifies that the line is not drawn.

→ I: nWidth defines the width of the lines.
→ I: crColor defines the color value of the Pen object that is used to draw the lines.

→ O/R: If the function is executed without errors, the function returns a value other than NULL.

→ N: If an error occurs while executing the function, the function returns the value NULL. To find out more about the error, you must call the Get-LastError function. This only works in Windows NT, however.

Support:

→ Windows NT 3.1 and higher
→ Windows 95 and higher
→ Windows CE 2.0 and higher

Header file: WINGDI.H

Library file: GDI32.LIB

17.1.20 Pen object

The Pen object contains line specifications relating to the width of the line, its appearance and its color. These specifications apply to all logical Pen objects that can be created using the CreatePen function. These Pen objects are used to draw lines and curves.

17.1.21 SelectObject

The SelectObject function links a pen, brush, font, bitmap and region to a device context. If a region is to be linked to a device context, this region is the update region. The update and the visible regions together form the clipping region. The clipping region is the area in which the drawing functions are supported:

```
HGDIOBJ SelectObject( HDC hdc, HGDIOBJ hgdiobj);
```

→ I: hdc is the handle to a device context. The objects specified in hgdiobj are linked to this device context. The device context gets information from the other object.

→ I: hgdiobj is the handle to the object, which is assigned to the device context.

→ O/R: If the function is executed without errors and the hgdi object is not a region, the function returns the handle to the old object, which is now no longer linked to the device context. If the object is a region, however, the function returns the value of a constant.

SIMPLEREGION means that the new region consists of one box. COMPLEXREGION means that the new region consists of a number of boxes.

NULLREGION means that the region has no size.

If an error occurs and the object is not a region, the function returns the value NULL, otherwise it returns the value of the GDI_ERROR constant.

Support:

→ Windows NT 3.1 and higher
→ Windows 95 and higher
→ Windows CE 1.0 and higher

Header file: WINGDI.H

Library file: GDI32.LIB

17.1.22   DeleteObject

The DeleteObject function deletes an object. These objects can be of the type logical Pen object, Brush object, Font object, Bitmap object, Region object or Palette object:

```
BOOL DeleteObject( HGDIOBJ hObject);
```

→ I: hObject is the handle to the object to be deleted.
→ O/R: If the function is executed without errors, the function returns the value NULL.
→ N: If the specified handle is not available or is incorporated into a device context, however, the return value is NULL. To find out more about the error, you can call the GetLastError function in Windows NT.

Support:

→ Windows NT 3.1 and higher
→ Windows 95 and higher
→ Windows CE 1.0 and higher

Header file: WINGDI.H

Library file: GDI32.LIB

17.1.23   CreateSolidBrush

The CreateSolidBrush function creates a Brush object containing only one color. Brush objects are generally used for backgrounds in drawing functions:

```
HBRUSH CreateSolidBrush( COLORREF crColor);
```

→ crColor is an RGB color value for the Brush object.

→ O/R: If the function is executed without errors, the function returns a value other than NULL.

→ N: If an error occurs while executing the function, the function returns the value NULL. To find out more about the error, call the `GetLastError` function. This only works in Windows NT, however.

Support:

→ Windows NT 3.1 and higher
→ Windows 95 and higher
→ Windows CE 1.0 and higher

Header file: WINGDI.H

Library file: GDI32.LIB

17.1.24 Brush object

A Brush object contains information about a color, a pattern or a bitmap for this pattern. Brush objects are often used to create a background using drawing functions. For example, you can create a Brush object containing information about a color using the `CreateSolidBrush` function.

17.1.25 TextOut

The `TextOut` function outputs a character string on a device context. This function uses the current font for the device context object. It also uses other device context object settings. These include the text alignment, the text color and the text background:

```
BOOL TextOut( HDC hdc, int nXStart, int nYStart,
              LPCTSTR lpString, int cbString);
```

→ I: `hdc` is the handle to the device context to which you want to write.
→ I: `nXStart` and `nYStart` specify the position at which the text is to be written. This position can be interpreted differently, depending on the text alignment. If the text is left-aligned, this position describes the top left corner of the start of the text. If it is centered, the text is arranged symmetrically around this position.
→ I: `lpString` is the text to be output.
→ I: `cbString` is the length of the text. This value specifies the number of characters in the text. In other words, the closing NULL character is not included here. This value is normally determined using the `lstrlen` function.
→ O/R: If the function is executed without errors, the function returns a value other than NULL.

→ N: If an error occurs while executing the function, the function returns the value NULL. To find out more about the error, you can call the `Get-LastError` function. This only works in Windows NT, however.

Support:

→ Windows NT 3.1 and higher
→ Windows 95 and higher
→ Windows CE not supported

Header file: WINGDI.H

Library file: GDI32.LIB

Support for ANSI and UNICODE in Windows and Windows NT

17.1.26 SetTextColor

The `SetTextColor` function sets the text color for a specific device context:

```
COLORREF SetTextColor( HDC hdc, COLORREF crColor);
```

→ I: `hdc` is the handle to a device context. The value for the text color is changed in this device context.
→ I: `crColor` is an RGB color value for the text color.
→ O/R: If the function is executed without errors, the function returns the value of the previous text color.
→ N: If an error occurs while executing the function, the function returns the value of the CLR_INVALID constant. You can use the `GetLastError` function in Windows NT to find out more about the error.

Support:

→ Windows NT 3.1 and higher
→ Windows 95 and higher
→ Windows CE 1.0 and higher

Header file: WINGDI.H

Library file: GDI32.LIB

17.1.27 SetBkColor

The `SetBkColor` function sets the background color of a device context. If this background color does not appear in this device context, it is set to the color that is most similar to it. This background color is used for displaying and printing text and for backgrounds in drawing functions:

```
COLORREF SetBkColor( HDC hdc, COLORREF crColor);
```

→ I: hdc is the handle to a device context. The background color of this device context is selected.

→ I: crColor is the color value that is set as the background color.

→ O/R: If the function is executed without errors, the function returns the value of the previous background color.

→ N: If an error occurs while executing the function, the function returns the value of the CLR_INVALID constant. You can find out more about the error in Windows NT using the GetLastError function.

Support:

→ Windows NT 3.1 and higher
→ Windows 95 and higher
→ Windows CE 1.0 and higher

Header file: WINGDI.H

Library file: GDI32.LIB

17.1.28 SetTextAlign

The SetTextAlign function sets the text alignment for a device context. Naturally, only the future text alignment is set:

```
UINT SetTextAlign( HDC hdc, UINT fMode);
```

→ hdc is the handle to a device context. The text alignment of this device context is set.

→ fMode defines how the text is to be aligned. One of the following constants can be specified for this. You can also specify the constants that can be used to change the current position. The following specifications apply to a specified box. This box is used by the DrawText function. The TextOut function only specifies the point, while the functions are interpreted differently there as appropriate.

TA_BASELINE specifies that the reference point is the base line.
TA_BOTTOM means that the reference point is at the bottom edge of the specified box.
TA_TOP defines that the reference point is at the top edge of the specified box.
TA_CENTER establishes that the reference point is at the horizontal center of the specified box. The text is arranged around the specified point when you use the TextOut function.
TA_LEFT specifies that the reference point is the specified left corner of the specified box. The position that was determined by TextOut is the

position at which the text aligns itself to the left.

TA_RIGHT states that the reference point is the specified right corner of the specified box. The text aligns itself to the right at the position defined by `TextOut`.

TA_NOUPDATECP means that the current position remains the same.

TA_UPDATECP defines that the current position is changed. It is also used as a reference point.

→ O/R: If the function is executed without errors, the function returns the value of the previous text alignment.
→ N: If an error occurs while executing the function, the function returns the value of the GDI_ERROR constant. You can find out more about the error in Windows NT using the `GetLastError` function.

Support:

→ Windows NT 3.1 and higher
→ Windows 95 and higher
→ Windows CE is not supported

Header file: WINGDI.H

Library file: GDI32.LIB

17.1.29   SetBkMode

The `SetBkMode` function sets an additional property for the background color:

```
int SetBkMode( HDC hdc, int iBkMode);
```

→ I: hdc is the handle to a device context. The setting for the background color of this device context is also defined.
→ I: iBkMode is the value of a constant. You can specify one of the following constants for this constant:

OPAQUE means that the background is filled with the background color before the background is written.

TRANSPARENT means that the background is not filled.

→ O/R: If the function is executed without errors, the function returns the value of the previous additional property for the background color.
→ N: If an error occurs while executing the function, the function returns the value 0. You can find out more about the error in Windows NT using the `GetLastError` function.

Support:

- → Windows NT 3.1 and higher
- → Windows 95 and higher
- → Windows CE 1.0 and higher

Header file: WINGDI.H

Library file: GDI32.LIB

17.1.30 RGB

The RGB macro determines the value of a color of the type COLORREF from three color components:

```
COLORREF RGB( BYTE bRed, BYTE bGreen, BYTE bBlue);
```

- → I: bRed, bGreen and bBlue specify the value of the color component.
- → O/R: The function returns the resultant color value.

Support:

- → Windows NT 3.1 and higher
- → Windows 95 and higher
- → Windows CE 1.0 and higher

Header file: WINGDI.H

17.1.31 CreateRectRgn

The CreateRectRgn function creates a Region object:

```
HRGN CreateRectRgn( int nLeftRect, int nTopRect,
                    int nRightRect, int nBottomRect);
```

- → I: nLeftRect, nTopRect, nRightRect and nBottomRect specify the size of the box. The box is specified relatively.
- → O/R: The function supplies a Region object as the return value.
- → N: If an error occurs while executing the function, the function returns the value NULL. You can find out more about the error in Windows NT using the GetLastError function.

Support:

→ Windows NT 3.1 and higher
→ Windows 95 and higher
→ Windows CE 2.0 and higher

Header file: WINGDI.H

Library file: GDI32.LIB

17.1.32 Region object

The region contains information about a certain area. Two types of regions can be defined. One is the visible region, which is assigned to the window. It is determined by the size of the window and the overlapped areas. You can also restrict this region even further using SetWindowRgn. There is also another region, which is assigned to the device context. This is the update region. The point of intersection, i.e. the clipping region, is formed from both regions. Every drawing function works out the new clipping region so as not to interfere with the area belonging to other applications.

17.1.33 CombineRgn

You can use the CombineRgn function to combine Region objects in various ways to form new Region objects:

```
int CombineRgn( HRGN hrgnDest, HRGN hrgnSrc1,
                HRGN hrgnSrc2, int fnCombineMode);
```

→ I: hrgnDest is the handle to the destination region. This region must exist before you call the CombineRgn function.
→ I: hrgnSrc1 and hrgnSrc2 are handles to regions. The destination object is formed from these two regions.
→ I: fnCombineMode specifies how the two regions are combined. You can specify one of the following constants for this value:

RGN_AND specifies that the newly formed region should be the logical AND from the two specified regions.
RGN_OR defines that the newly formed region should be the logical OR from the two specified regions.
RGN_XOR specifies that the newly formed region should be the logical XOR from the two specified regions.
RGN_COPY states that the hrgnSrc1 region is to be copied.

→ O/R: The function supplies the value of a constant as the return value. You can use the values of the following constants:

NULLREGION specifies that the newly formed region is empty.
SIMPLEREGION means that the newly formed region is a simple box.
COMPLEXREGION defines that the newly formed region is more than a simple box.
ERROR specifies that no region was created because an error occurred.

Support:

→ Windows NT 3.1 and higher
→ Windows 95 and higher
→ Windows CE 1.0 and higher

Header file: WINGDI.H

Library file: GDI32.LIB

17.1.34 SetWindowRgn

The SetWindowRgn function sets a region for a specific window. This is combined with the visible region, which is not overlapped by the window:

```
int SetWindowRgn( HWND hWnd, HRGN hRgn, BOOL bRedraw);
```

→ hWnd is the handle to the window containing the region to be set.
→ hRgn is the handle to the region to be set.
→ bRedraw specifies that the window is to be redrawn after the region has been set. The value TRUE here means that the window is redrawn, while FALSE indicates that the window is not redrawn.
→ O/R: If the function is executed without errors, the function returns a value other than NULL.
→ N: If an error occurs while executing the function, the function returns the value NULL. You can use the GetLastError function to find out more about the error.

Support:

→ Windows NT 3.51 and higher
→ Windows 95 and higher
→ Windows CE not supported.

Header file: WINUSER.H

Library file: USER32.LIB

17.1.35 GetStockObject

The `GetStockObject` function supplies the handle for a predefined object and for Pen, Brush, Font, and Palette objects:

```
HGDIOBJ GetStockObject( int fnObject);
```

→ I: `fnObject` is the value of a constant. This constant specifies which handle is to be returned by which object.

WHITE_BRUSH specifies that a handle to a white Brush object is returned.
BLACK_BRUSH means that a handle to a black Brush object is returned.
DKGRAY_BRUSH defines that a handle to a dark gray Brush object is returned.
GRAY_BRUSH means that a handle to a gray Brush object is returned.
LTGRAY_BRUSH specifies that a handle to a light gray Brush object is returned.
DC_BRUSH establishes that a handle to a defined Brush object is returned. The default color is white. You can set the color using the `SetDCBrushColor` function.
NULL_BRUSH means that a handle to a predefined Brush object is returned. Nothing is drawn wherever this Brush object is used.
WHITE_PEN means that a handle to a white Pen object is returned.
BLACK_PEN specifies that a handle to a black Pen object is returned.
DC_PEN defines that a handle to a predefined Pen object is returned. You can set this Pen object using the SetDCPenColor function.
ANSI_FIXED_FONT means that a handle to a Font object is returned.
ANSI_VAR_FONT specifies that a handle to a Font object is returned. This font is a proportional font.
OEM_FIXED_FONT means that a handle to a Font object is returned. This is the extended DOS character set with block graphics. This character set is provided for downward compatibility. It is a non-proportional font.
SYSTEM_FONT defines that a handle to a Font object is returned. This font is used to draw menus and predefined dialog boxes.
SYSTEM_FIXED_FONT means that a handle to a Font object is returned. This font is provided for Windows versions that are older than Windows 3.0.
DEFAULT_GUI_FONT specifies that a handle to a Font object is returned.
DEFAULT_PALETTE means that a handle to a Palette object containing the default system colors is returned.

→ O/R: The handle to the GDI object is returned.

TAKE THAT!

→ N: If an error occurs while executing the function, the function returns the value NULL. You can use the `GetLastError` function to find out more about the error.

Support:

→ Windows NT 3.1 and higher
→ Windows 95 and higher
→ Windows CE 1.0 and higher

Header file: WINGDI.H

Library file: GDI32.LIB

17.1.36 DrawText

The `DrawText` function displays text on the screen. A box is defined for this on the screen:

```
int DrawText( HDC hDC, LPCTSTR lpString, int nCount,
              LPRECT lpRect, UINT uFormat);
```

→ I: `hDC` is the handle to the device context in which the text is to be displayed.
→ I: `lpString` is the text to be displayed.
→ I: `nCount` is the number of characters in the text. This value must be –1 if the string ends with a NULL character. The function then determines the string automatically.
→ I: `lpRect` is a pointer to a structure of the type RECT. This structure contains data relating to the box in which the text is to be displayed.
→ I: `uFormat` specifies how the text is displayed in the box. Any combination of the following constants can be used here.

DT_BOTTOM defines that the text is aligned at the bottom of the box. This constant must be combined with the DT_SINGLELINE constant.
DT_CALCRECT instructs the function to calculate the size of the box for a multi-line text.
DT_CENTER specifies that the text is displayed centered horizontally in the box.
DT_EDITCONTROL means that the text is displayed in exactly the same way as in a *Multi-Line Edit Control*.
DT_END_ELLIPSES/ DT_PATH_ELLIPSES defines that the text is adapted according to the size of the box. To do this, DT_MODIFYSTRING must also be specified.
DT_EXPANDTABS expands the tab characters. The default length of a tab

character is 8.

DT_EXTERNAL_LEADING indicates that the height of the text is specified with *external leading*.

DT_INTERNAL means that the system font is used to change the text settings.

DT_LEFT specifies that the text is left-aligned.

DT_MODIFYSTRING specifies that the text is adapted to suit the display area. This constant has no effect if DT_END_ELLIPSES or DT_PATH_ELLIPSES was specified.

DT_NOCLIP specifies that the text is drawn without clipping.

DT_NOPREFIX means that an & is no longer used for underlining, but is displayed on the screen.

DT_RIGHT specifies that the text is aligned at the right edge of the box.

DT_SINGLELINE defines that the text is displayed in one line.

DT_TABSTOP specifies that the number of characters is set for a tab stop.

DT_TOP establishes that the text is aligned at the top edge of the box.

DT_VCENTERS specifies that the text is centered vertically.

DT_WORDBREAK means that words are hyphenated automatically.

DT_WORD_ELLIPSES specifies that words are not written out fully if they do not fit in the box. An ellipse is then added.

➡ O/R: If the function is executed without errors, the function returns the height of the text.

➡ N: If an error occurs while executing the function, the function returns the value NULL. You can find out more about the error in Windows NT using the GetLastError function.

Support:

➡ Windows NT 3.1 and higher
➡ Windows 95 and higher
➡ Windows CE 1.0 and higher

Header file: WINUSER.H

Library file: USER32.LIB

Support for ANSI and UNICODE in Windows NT

17.2 Examples

17.2.1 Finding a graphics area in the WM_PAINT message and drawing something in it

A device context is determined if the WM_PAINT message has to be processed. However, this device context only describes the region that must be redrawn. A box and an ellipse are then drawn in this device context (see Figure 17.1). The device context is then released.

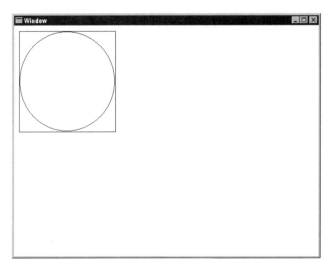

Figure 17.1 *The application after you start it*

The source code

```
#include <windows.h>

LRESULT CALLBACK WndProc (HWND, UINT, WPARAM, LPARAM);

int APIENTRY WinMain(HINSTANCE hInstance,
                     HINSTANCE hPrevInstance,
                     LPSTR     lpCmdLine,
                     int       nCmdShow )
{
   WNDCLASS WndClass;
   WndClass.style = 0;
   WndClass.cbClsExtra = 0;
   WndClass.cbWndExtra = 0;
   WndClass.lpfnWndProc = WndProc;
```

```
WndClass.hInstance = hInstance;
WndClass.hbrBackground = (HBRUSH) (COLOR_WINDOW+1);
WndClass.hCursor = LoadCursor (NULL, IDC_ARROW);
WndClass.hIcon = LoadIcon (NULL, IDI_APPLICATION);
WndClass.lpszMenuName = 0;
WndClass.lpszClassName = "WinProg";

RegisterClass(&WndClass);

HWND hWindow;
hWindow = CreateWindow("WinProg","Window",
                       WS_OVERLAPPEDWINDOW,
                       0,0,600,460,NULL,NULL,
                       hInstance, NULL);

ShowWindow (hWindow, nCmdShow);

UpdateWindow (hWindow);

MSG Message;
while (GetMessage(&Message, NULL, 0, 0))
{
    DispatchMessage(&Message);
}


return (Message.wParam);
}

LRESULT CALLBACK WndProc (HWND hWnd, UINT uiMessage,
                          WPARAM wParam,LPARAM lParam)
{
    switch(uiMessage)
    {
        case WM_PAINT:
            HDC hdc;
            PAINTSTRUCT ps;
            hdc = BeginPaint (hWnd, &ps);

            Rectangle (hdc, 10, 10, 200, 200);

            Ellipse (hdc, 11, 11, 199, 199);
```

```
        EndPaint (hWnd, &ps);
        return 0;
    case WM_DESTROY:
        PostQuitMessage(0);
        return 0;
    default:
        return DefWindowProc (hWnd, uiMessage,
                                wParam, lParam);
    }
}
```

17.2.2   Creating and assigning Pen and Brush objects

Description

A Pen object and a Brush object are created in the WM_PAINT message. Both are assigned to the device context that was created by the window. The old objects of the device context are backed up and reassigned at the end. You can use Pen and Brush objects to change the character color and fill color of various drawing functions (see Figure 17.2).

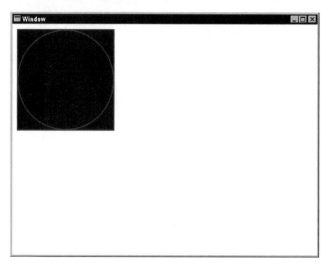

Figure 17.2 *The application after you start it*

The source code

```
#include <windows.h>
```

```
LRESULT CALLBACK WndProc (HWND, UINT, WPARAM, LPARAM);

int APIENTRY WinMain(HINSTANCE hInstance,
                     HINSTANCE hPrevInstance,
                     LPSTR     lpCmdLine,
                     int       nCmdShow )

    WNDCLASS WndClass;
    WndClass.style = 0;
    WndClass.cbClsExtra = 0;
    WndClass.cbWndExtra = 0;
    WndClass.lpfnWndProc = WndProc;
    WndClass.hInstance = hInstance;
    WndClass.hbrBackground = (HBRUSH) (COLOR_WINDOW+1);
    WndClass.hCursor = LoadCursor (NULL, IDC_ARROW);
    WndClass.hIcon = LoadIcon (NULL, IDI_APPLICATION);
    WndClass.lpszMenuName = 0;
    WndClass.lpszClassName = "WinProg";

    RegisterClass(&WndClass);

    HWND hWindow;
    hWindow = CreateWindow("WinProg","Window",
                          WS_OVERLAPPEDWINDOW,
                          0,0,600,460,NULL,NULL,
                          hInstance, NULL);

    ShowWindow (hWindow, nCmdShow);

    UpdateWindow (hWindow);

    MSG Message;
    while (GetMessage(&Message, NULL, 0, 0))
    {
        DispatchMessage(&Message);
    }

    return (Message.wParam);
}


LRESULT CALLBACK WndProc (HWND hWnd, UINT uiMessage,
```

```
                                     WPARAM wParam,LPARAM lParam)
{
   switch(uiMessage)
   {
      case WM_PAINT:
         HDC hdc;
         PAINTSTRUCT ps;
         hdc = BeginPaint (hWnd, &ps);

         HPEN hPen, hPenPrevious;
         HGDIOBJ hGDI;
         hPen = CreatePen (PS_SOLID, 2, RGB(255,0,0));
         hGDI = SelectObject (hdc, HGDIOBJ (hPen));

         hPenPrevious = HPEN (hGDI);
         HBRUSH hBrush, hBrushPrevious;
         hBrush = CreateSolidBrush ( RGB(0,0,255));
         hGDI = SelectObject (hdc, hBrush);
         hBrushPrevious = HBRUSH (hGDI);

         Rectangle (hdc, 10, 10, 200, 200);

         Ellipse (hdc, 11, 11, 199, 199);

         SelectObject (hdc, hPenPrevious);
         DeleteObject (hPen);
         SelectObject (hdc, hBrushPrevious);
         DeleteObject (hBrushPrevious);
         EndPaint (hWnd, &ps);

         return 0;
      case WM_DESTROY:
         PostQuitMessage(0);
         return 0;
      default:
         return DefWindowProc (hWnd, uiMessage,
                                 wParam, lParam);
   }
}
```

17.2.3   Displaying text

We want to display text, which is assigned a color and a background color. The text is aligned and has a font type (see Figure 17.3).

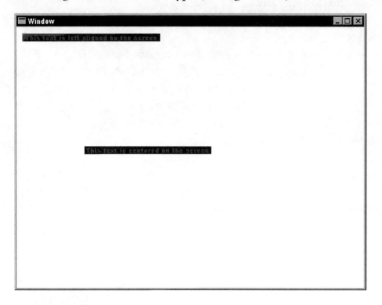

Figure 17.3   *The application after you start it*

The source code

```
#include <windows.h>

LRESULT CALLBACK WndProc (HWND, UINT, WPARAM, LPARAM);

int APIENTRY WinMain(HINSTANCE hInstance,
                     HINSTANCE hPrevInstance,
                     LPSTR     lpCmdLine,
                     int       nCmdShow )
{
   WNDCLASS WndClass;
   WndClass.style = 0;
   WndClass.cbClsExtra = 0;
   WndClass.cbWndExtra = 0;
   WndClass.lpfnWndProc = WndProc;
   WndClass.hInstance = hInstance;
   WndClass.hbrBackground = (HBRUSH) (COLOR_WINDOW+1);
   WndClass.hCursor = LoadCursor (NULL, IDC_ARROW);
   WndClass.hIcon = LoadIcon (NULL, IDI_APPLICATION);
```

```
            WndClass.lpszMenuName = 0;
            WndClass.lpszClassName = "WinProg";

            RegisterClass(&WndClass);

            HWND hWindow;
            hWindow = CreateWindow("WinProg","Window",
                              WS_OVERLAPPEDWINDOW,
                              0,0,600,460,NULL,NULL,
                              hInstance, NULL);

            ShowWindow (hWindow, nCmdShow);

            UpdateWindow (hWindow);

            MSG Message;
            while (GetMessage(&Message, NULL, 0, 0))
            {
               DispatchMessage(&Message);
            }
            return (Message.wParam);
      }
      LRESULT CALLBACK WndProc (HWND hWnd, UINT uiMessage,
                                WPARAM wParam,LPARAM lParam)
      {
            switch(uiMessage)
            {
               case WM_PAINT:
                  HDC hdc;
                  PAINTSTRUCT ps;
                  hdc = BeginPaint (hWnd, &ps);

                  SetTextColor (hdc, RGB(255,0,0));
                  SetBkColor (hdc, RGB(0,0,255));
                  SetTextAlign (hdc, TA_LEFT);


                  SelectObject (hdc,
                              GetStockObject
                              (SYSTEM_FIXED_FONT));
                  char *Text;
                  Text = new char[80];
```

```
        lstrcpy (Text,
                "This text is left-aligned on the
                screen.");

        TextOut (hdc, 10,10, Text, lstrlen(Text));

        lstrcpy (Text, "This text is centered on the
                screen.");

        RECT rect;
        rect.left = 40;
        rect.top = 10;
        rect.right = 400;
        rect.bottom = 400;

        DrawText (hdc, Text, -1, &rect,
                DT_CENTER | DT_VCENTER |
                DT_SINGLELINE);

        delete [] Text;

        EndPaint (hWnd, &ps);

        return 0;
    case WM_DESTROY:
        PostQuitMessage(0);
        return 0;
    default:
        return DefWindowProc (hWnd, uiMessage,
                            wParam, lParam);
    }
}
```

17.2.4   Using regions

We want to create a window region and assign it to the window. All the drawing functions will only be executed in this area. It makes no difference whether the drawing functions refer to the device context of the *non-client area* or to the client area of the window because both are linked to the window. As a result, each drawing function will only draw in the area in which it is authorized to draw. A round window appears on the screen (see Figure 17.4).

Figure 17.4   *The application after you start it (The gray part is the background)*

The source code

```
#include <windows.h>

int Status1;

LRESULT CALLBACK WndProc (HWND, UINT, WPARAM, LPARAM);

int APIENTRY WinMain(HINSTANCE hInstance,
                     HINSTANCE hPrevInstance,
                     LPSTR     lpCmdLine,
                     int       nCmdShow )
{
   WNDCLASS WndClass;
   WndClass.style = 0;
   WndClass.cbClsExtra = 0;
   WndClass.cbWndExtra = 0;
   WndClass.lpfnWndProc = WndProc;
   WndClass.hInstance = hInstance;
   WndClass.hbrBackground = (HBRUSH) (COLOR_WINDOW+1);
   WndClass.hCursor = LoadCursor (NULL, IDC_ARROW);
   WndClass.hIcon = LoadIcon (NULL, IDI_APPLICATION);
```

```
    WndClass.lpszMenuName = 0;
    WndClass.lpszClassName = "WinProg";

    RegisterClass(&WndClass);

    HWND hWindow;
    hWindow = CreateWindow("WinProg","Window",
                           WS_OVERLAPPEDWINDOW,
                           0,0,600,460,NULL,NULL,
                           hInstance, NULL);

    ShowWindow (hWindow, nCmdShow);

    UpdateWindow (hWindow);

    HRGN hRgn;
    hRgn = CreateEllipticRgn (40, 0, 240, 200);
    SetWindowRgn (hWindow, hRgn, TRUE);

    SetTimer (hWindow, 99, 10, 0);

    MSG Message;
    while (GetMessage(&Message, NULL, 0, 0))
    {
       DispatchMessage(&Message);
    }

    return (Message.wParam);
}

LRESULT CALLBACK WndProc (HWND hWnd, UINT uiMessage,
                          WPARAM wParam,LPARAM lParam)
{
    switch(uiMessage)
    {
       case WM_PAINT:
          HDC hdc;
          PAINTSTRUCT ps;
          hdc = BeginPaint (hWnd, &ps);

          SelectObject (hdc,
                        CreateSolidBrush (RGB(0,0,255)));
```

```
            Rectangle (hdc,0,0,400,400);

            EndPaint (hWnd, &ps);
            return 0;
        case WM_DESTROY:
            PostQuitMessage(0);
            return 0;
        default:
            return DefWindowProc (hWnd, uiMessage,
                                  wParam, lParam);
    }
}
```

Win32 API: File management

18.1 Win32 API functions, structures, messages, and objects for file management

The Win32 API provides a number of functions for file management. It is therefore not dependent on the file system used in Windows.

There are essentially three file systems: the FAT file system, the Protected FAT file system, and the NTFS file system.

The FAT file system is the oldest and most frequently used file system. It can also be used equally well for hard disks. This file system is supported by DOS, Windows and OS/2. A file name can be up to eight characters long.

The Protected FAT file system can be used for floppy disk drives and hard disks. It is compatible with the FAT file system. File names in the Protected FAT file system can be 255 characters long using the NULL character. Directory paths can contain 260 characters using the NULL character.

The NTFS file system is designed for Windows NT. It also supports file names of 255 characters. In addition, the file system has a number of new features, which allow you to assign various properties to the files.

The file functions work in the usual way. If a certain file is to be accessed, an object is created for it. This file object can inform another program, for example, that it can no longer access the file because an object already exists for this file. All file functions need these file objects in order to execute actions using the files. This means that a file object, which controls all access to this file, is created for accessing a file.

Functions, structures, messages, and objects	Meaning
CreateFile	The CreateFile function creates or opens a file. It returns a file handle to this file, i.e. it creates a file object
CloseHandle	The CloseHandle function deletes a file object
ReadFile	The ReadFile function reads data from a file by specifying the file object
WriteFile	The WriteFile function writes data to a file by specifying the file object
CopyFile	The CopyFile function copies a file
DeleteFile	The DeleteFile function deletes a file
MoveFile	The MoveFile function renames a file or directory

Table 18.1 *Win32 API functions, structures, messages, and objects for file management*

18.1.1 CreateFile

The CreateFile function creates an object for a file. This object ensures that no other object can be created for this file. It allows the other functions, such as ReadFile and WriteFile, to access the file:

```
HANDLE CreateFile( LPCTSTR lpFileName,
                   DWORD dwDesiredAccess,
                   DWORD dwShareMode,
                   LPSECURITY_ATTRIBUTES
                   lpSecurityAttributes,
                   DWORD dwCreationDisposition,
                   DWORD dwFlagsAndAttributes,
                   HANDLE hTemplateFile);
```

→ I: lpFileName is the file name. A file object is created from this file.
→ I: dwDesiredAccess defines how the file can be used. A combination of the following constants is specified for this:

GENERIC_WRITE means that data can be written to the file.
GENERIC_READ means that data can be read from the file.

0 means that information about a device can be obtained without contacting the device.

→ I: dwShareMode defines whether more than one handle to a file object can be issued. This property is defined by a combination of the following constants:

FILE_SHARE_READ means that a number of handles to the object can be issued by a read access operation.
FILE_SHARE_WRITE means that a number of handles to the object can be issued by a write access operation.

→ I: lpSecurityAttributes determines which security attributes are set for the returned object. This is specified by a structure of the type SECURITY_ATTRIBUTES.

→ I: dwCreationDisposition specifies which action is to be performed if the file exists or does not exist. This parameter comprises one of the following values:

CREATE_NEW specifies that a new file is created. This function returns an error if the file already exists.
CREATE_ALWAYS means that a new file is always created.
OPEN_EXISTING defines that the file is only opened if it exists.
OPEN_ALWAYS means that the file is always opened.
TRUNCATE_EXIST establishes that the file is opened and is then reduced to 0 bytes. This function returns an error if the file does not exist.

→ I/O: dwFlagsAndAttributes specifies the file attributes. All combinations of the following constants can be used:

FILE_ATTRIBUTE_ARCHIVE has the archive bit set. Used for marking files that have been backed up.
FILE_ATTRIBUTE_HIDDEN defines that the file is hidden.
FILE_ATTRIBUTE_NORMAL specifies that the file has the standard attributes indicating a normal file or directory.
FILE_ATTRIBUTE_OFFLINE specifies that the data in this file is not available immediately.
FILE_ATTRIBUTE_READ_ONLY states that the file is a read-only file.
FILE_ATTRIBUTE_SYSTEM means that the file is part of the operating system or is used by the operating system.
FILE_ATTRIBUTE_TEMPORARY indicates that the file is a temporary file.

The following additional combinations are also possible:

FILE_FLAG_WRITE_THROUGH specifies that data is written directly to the hard disk. Of course, the data is first written to the *cache memory.*
FILE_FLAG_OVERLAPPED means that operations need a certain amount of time to access the file using a file object.
FILE_FLAG_NO_BUFFERING specifies that the system opens the file without buffering and without using the *cache memory.*
FILE_FLAG_RANDOM_ACCESS means that the file will be accessed in a random fashion.
FILE_FLAG_SEQUENTIAL_SCAN specifies that the entire file is read in one operation.
FILE_FLAG_DELETE_ON_CLOSE means that the file is deleted as soon as all the handles to the file have been closed.
FILE_FLAG_BACKUP_SEMANTIC means that the file was opened or created for a backup.
FILE_POSIX_SEMATICS defines that the file is managed in accordance with *POSIX rules.*
FILE_FLAG_OPEN_REPARSE_POINT determines the behavior of the *reparse point.*
FILE_FLAG_OPEN_NO_RECALL defines how data in the file is stored.

You can also specify a combination of the following constants:

SECURITY_ANONYMOUS indicates that the client is anonymous.
SECURITY_IDENTIFICATION means that the client must identify itself.
SECURITY_IMPERSONATION establishes that the client must be on the *Impersonate level.*
SECURITY_DELEGATION specifies that the client must be on the *Delegation level.*
SECURITY_CONTEXT_TRACKING specifies that security tracking is dynamic, otherwise it is static.
SECURITY_EFFECTIVE_ONLY indicates that only the enabled client aspects are visible for the server.

→ I: Defines a handle for a *template file.*
→ O/R: If the function can be executed without errors, it returns the handle to a file object. If the file is overwritten, the `GetLastError` function returns the value of the ERROR_ALREADY_EXISTS constant.
→ N: If an error occurs while executing the function, it returns the value of the INVALID_FILE_ HANDLE constant. You can get more information on the error using the `GetLastError` function.

Support:

→ Windows NT 3.1 and higher
→ Windows 95 and higher
→ Windows CE 1.0 and higher

Header file: WINBASE.H

Library file: KERNEL32.LIB

Support for ANSI and UNICODE in Windows NT.

18.1.2   CloseHandle

The CloseHandle function can close an open file object. In other words, the function ensures that the file object can issue a new handle:

```
BOOL CloseHandle( HANDLE hObject);
```

→ I: hObject is the handle to the file object to be closed.
→ O/R: The function supplies a value other than NULL as the return value if no errors occurred while executing the function.
→ N: If an error occurs while executing the function, however, it returns the value NULL.

Support:

→ Windows NT 3.1 and higher
→ Windows 95 and higher
→ Windows CE 1.0 and higher

Header file: WINBASE.H

Library file: KERNEL32.LIB

18.1.3   ReadFile

The ReadFile function reads data from a file by specifying a file object:

```
BOOL ReadFile( HANDLE hFile, LPVOID lpBuffer,
               DWORD nNumberOfBytesToRead,
               LPDWORD lpNumberOfBytesRead,
               LPOVERLAPPED lpOverlapped);
```

→ I: hFile is the handle to the file object from which you want to read data. The file object must have been created using the GENERIC_READ constant.
→ I: lpBuffer is a pointer to the memory to which you want to read in the file.

→ I: nNumberOfBytesToRead specifies the number of bytes to be read from the file.

→ I: lpNumberOfBytesRead specifies the number of bytes that were read from the file.

→ I: lpOverlapped is a pointer to a structure of the type OVERLAPPED. You can enter an offset in the file, for example, in this structure. The file object must have been created using the FILE_FLAG_OVERLAPPED constant.

→ O/R: The function supplies a value other than NULL as the return value if no errors occurred while executing the function.

→ N: If errors occur while executing the function, however, it returns the value NULL.

Support:

→ Windows NT 3.1 and higher

→ Windows 95 and higher

→ Windows CE 1.0 and higher

Header file: WINBASE.H

Library file: KERNEL32.LIB

18.1.4   WriteFile

The WriteFile function writes data to a file, which was specified using a file object:

```
BOOL WriteFile( HANDLE hFile, LPCVOID lpBuffer,
                DWORD nNumberOfBytesToWrite,
                LPDWORD lpNumberOfBytesWritten,
                LPOVERLAPPED lpOverlapped);
```

→ I: hFile is a handle to a file object. The file, which is represented by this object, is the file from which data is read. The file object must have been created using the GENERIC_WRITE constant.

→ I: lpBuffer is a pointer to a buffer from which the data is written.

→ I: nNumberOfBytesToWrite is the number of bytes to be written.

→ I: lpNumberOfBytesWritten is the number of bytes that were written.

→ I: lpOverlapped is a pointer to a structure of the type OVERLAPPED. You can use this structure to enter an offset in the file. The file object must have been created using the FILE_FLAG_OVERLAPPED constant.

→ O/R: The function supplies a value other than NULL as the return value if no errors occurred while executing the function.

→ N: If errors occur while executing the function, however, it returns the value NULL.

Support:

→ Windows NT 3.1 and higher
→ Windows 95 and higher
→ Windows CE 1.0 and higher

Header file: WINBASE.H

Library file: KERNEL32.LIB

18.1.5 CopyFile

The CopyFile function copies a file by creating another file and storing the same contents there:

```
BOOL CopyFile( LPCTSTR lpExistingFileName,
               LPCTSTR lpNewFileName, BOOL bFailIfExists);
```

→ I: lpExistingFileName is the name of the file to be copied.
→ I: lpNewFileName is the name of the new file to be created for the copy operation.
→ I: bFailIfExists determines how the function should behave if the file specified by lpNewFileName already exists.

TRUE specifies that an error is output if the file already exists.
FALSE specifies that the file is overwritten.

→ O/R: The function supplies a value other than NULL as the return value if no errors occurred while executing the function.
→ N: If errors occur while executing the function, however, it returns the value NULL.

Support:

→ Windows NT 3.1 and higher
→ Windows 95 and higher
→ Windows CE 1.0 and higher

Header file: WINBASE.H

Library file: KERNEL32.LIB

Support for ANSI and UNICODE in Windows NT

18.1.6   DeleteFile

The `DeleteFile` function deletes a file:

```
BOOL DeleteFile( LPCTSTR lpFileName);
```

→ I: `lpFileName` is the name of the file to be deleted.
→ O/R: The function supplies a value other than NULL as the return value if no errors occurred while executing the function.
→ N: If errors occur while executing the function, however, it returns the value NULL.

Support:

→ Windows NT 3.1 and higher
→ Windows 95 and higher
→ Windows CE 1.0 and higher

Header file: WINBASE.H

Library file: KERNEL32.LIB

→ Support for ANSI and UNICODE in Windows NT

18.1.7   MoveFile

The `MoveFile` function renames a file or directory:

```
BOOL MoveFile( LPCTSTR lpExistingFileName,
               LPCTSTR lpNewFileName);
```

→ I: `lpExistingFileName` is the name of the file or a directory. The specified file or directory is renamed.
→ I: `lpNewFileName` is the new name for the file or directory.
→ O/R: The function supplies a value other than NULL as the return value if no errors occurred while executing the function.
→ N: If errors occur while executing the function, however, it returns the value NULL.

Support:

→ Windows NT 3.1 and higher
→ Windows 95 and higher
→ Windows CE 1.0 and higher

Header file: WINBASE.H

Library file: KERNEL32.LIB

→ Support for ANSI and UNICODE in Windows NT

18.2.1   Creating a simple file and filling it with data

This example stores an int value in a file:

```
#include <windows.h>

int APIENTRY WinMain(HINSTANCE hInstance,
                     HINSTANCE hPrevInstance,
                     LPSTR     lpCmdLine,
                     int       nCmdShow )
{
   HANDLE hFile;
   int Data;
   Data = 1;
   DWORD Readd;
   hFile = CreateFile ("c:\\int.dat", GENERIC_WRITE, 0,
                       NULL, CREATE_ALWAYS, NULL, NULL);
   WriteFile (hFile,&Data,sizeof(Data),&Readd,NULL);
   CloseHandle (hFile);

   return 0;
}
```

18.2.2   Opening a simple file and reading data from it

This example opens the int.dat file, reads an int value from it and displays it. For this purpose, a device context is determined for the entire screen rather than for a window:

```
#include <windows.h>

int APIENTRY WinMain(HINSTANCE hInstance,
                     HINSTANCE hPrevInstance,
                     LPSTR     lpCmdLine,
                     int       nCmdShow )
{
   HANDLE hFile;
   int Data;
   DWORD Readd;
   hFile = CreateFile ("c:\\int.dat", GENERIC_READ, 0,
                       NULL, OPEN_EXISTING, NULL, NULL);
   ReadFile (hFile,&Data,sizeof(Data),&Readd,NULL);
```

```
        CloseHandle (hFile);

        HDC hdc;
        hdc = GetDC (NULL);

        char *Text;
        Text = new char[20];

        itoa (Data, Text, 10);

        TextOut (hdc, 10, 10, Text, lstrlen (Text));

        delete [] Text;

        ReleaseDC (NULL, hdc);


        return 0;
}
```

Predefined window classes

19.1 General information

There are a number of predefined window classes in Windows that are mainly used for control elements. All window classes also have their own specific window function. The most important class is called BUTTON and is used, as the name suggests, to set buttons. The window classes can vary from one Windows version to the next. However, the proportions are always the same in the standard Windows versions so as to guarantee downward compatibility.

All windows that are created by a predefined window class are designed in such a way that they deliver a message to the parent window for an event. This message is generally called WM_COMMAND for all control elements.

Of course, you can also send messages to the control elements and this allows you to simulate working with control elements. You can also do this by sending system messages or by sending a WM_COMMAND message to the parent window.

You can use the WM_CTLCOLOR message to change the color of specific objects that were created by predefined window classes.

Window class	Meaning
BUTTON	The window can be a push button, a check box, a radio button, an owner-drawn button or a group box
EDIT	The window is an edit field
LISTBOX	The window is a list box
STATIC	The window is a text field

Table 19.1 *Important window classes*

19.1.1 BUTTON

General information

There are five different types of buttons, namely (see Figure 19.1):

1. Push buttons
2. Check boxes
3. Radio buttons
4. Owner-drawn buttons
5. Group boxes

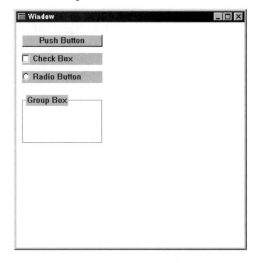

Figure 19.1 *The various buttons*

Push button

A push button is a rectangular box with a label or a picture. You can click this box to trigger an action.

Check box

A check box is a square box with a label or a picture shown beside it. You can select the check box and use it when you have the option of selecting one or more objects.

Radio button

A radio button is a round field with a label or a bitmap shown to the side. When you select a radio button, all the other related radio buttons should automatically revert to "not selected".

Owner-drawn buttons

An owner-drawn button is a field that allows you to draw a button.

Group box

A group box is a box containing a group of control elements. This is used for visual presentation. Text is displayed in the top left corner.

Styles

BS_PUSHBUTTON specifies that the BUTTON window object that was created looks like a push button and also behaves like one.

BS_DEFPUSHBUTTON means that the BUTTON window object that was created looks like a push button and behaves as if it were the default push button.

BS_CHECKBOX specifies that the BUTTON window object that was created looks like a check box.

BS_AUTOCHECKBOX specifies that the BUTTON window object that was created looks like a check box and no other check boxes in the same group can be selected if this check box is selected.

BS_RADIOBUTTON defines that the BUTTON window object that was created looks like a radio button.

BS_AUTORADIOBUTTON specifies that the BUTTON window object that was created looks like a radio button and no other radio buttons can be selected if this radio button is selected.

BS_LEFTTEXT means that the text appears on the left side for radio buttons and check boxes.

19

BS_OWNERDRAWN establishes that the window that was created behaves like a button, whereby the button must be drawn. The WM_DRAWITEM message is sent to the parent window for this purpose.

BS_GROUPBOX means that the window that was created behaves like a group box. Text can appear in the top left corner.

BS_3STATE means that the window that was created behaves like a check box. Three states can be defined for the check box.

BS_AUTO3STATE specifies that the window that was created behaves like a check box with three states, where no other check boxes can be selected if this check box is selected.

BS_USERBUTTON works in the same way as BS_OWNERDRAWN. The reason for this is that BS_USERBUTTON is still only relevant for 16-bit programs.

BS_BITMAP specifies that the button shows a bitmap.

BS_BOTTOM establishes that the text is aligned at the bottom.

BS_CENTER defines that the text is centered.

BS_RIGHT means that the text is right-aligned.

BS_ICON specifies that the button shows an icon.

BS_FLAT specifies that the button is displayed as a two-dimensional button.

BS_MULTILINE specifies that the button text appears in a number of lines if it is too long.

BS_NOTIFY means that the button sends BM_SETFOCUS, BM_KILLFOCUS and BM_DBLCLICK to the parent window. The BN_CLICKED message is always sent.

BS_PUSHLIKE specifies that other buttons look like push buttons. These buttons include check buttons, radio buttons and buttons with three states.

BS_RIGHTBUTTON means the same as BS_LEFTTEXT.

BS_TEXT specifies that the button contains text.

BS_TOP specifies that the text is aligned at the top.

BS_VCENTER specifies that the text appears in the vertical center of the button box.

Messages from the parent window to the button

BM_CLICK

The BM_CLICK message is sent to the button. This triggers WM_LBUTTONDOWN and WM_LBUTTONUP and a BN_CLICKED message is sent to the parent window. This message therefore simulates a button click. Otherwise, this message is not significant, it is intended only for simulation:

```
BM_CLICK
wParam = 0;
lParam = 0;
```

Support:

→ WinNT 3.1 and higher
→ Win95 and higher
→ WinCE 1.0 and higher

Header file: WINUSER.H

BM_GETCHECK

The BM_GETCHECK message is sent to the button window and returns a value indicating whether or not the button is selected. This only happens with radio buttons and check boxes:

```
BM_GETCHECK
wParam = 0;
lParam = 0;
```

→ O/R: This message returns the following constants.
BST_CHECKED specifies that the button is selected.
BST_UNCHECKED defines that the button is not selected.
BST_INTERMEDIATE specifies that the button is grayed.

Support:

→ WinNT 3.1 and higher
→ Win95 and higher
→ WinCE 1.0 and higher

Header file: WINUSER.H

BM_GETIMAGE

The BM_GETIMAGE message is sent in order to get a handle to the bitmap or icon that was associated with the button:

```
BM_GETIMAGE
wParam = (WPARAM) fImageType;
lParam = 0;
```

→ I: fImageType specifies whether an icon or a bitmap is to be returned.
IMAGE_BITMAP means that a handle to a bitmap is to be returned.
IMAGE_ICON specifies that a handle to an icon is to be returned.

→ O/R: If a bitmap or an icon was found, the handle to this bitmap or icon is returned.

→ N: If no bitmap or icon exists, the value NULL is returned.

Support:

→ WinNT 4.0 and higher
→ Win95 and higher
→ WinCE not supported

Header file: WINUSER.H

BM_GETSTATE

The BM_GETSTATE message is sent in order to find out the status of a button or check box:

```
BM_GETSTATE
wParam = 0;
lParam = 0;
```

→ O/R: A value indicating the status of the button is returned. The status of the button is determined using a bit mask.

0x0003
BST_CHECKED specifies that the button is selected.
BST_UNCHECKED specifies that the button is not selected.
BST_INTERMEDIATE indicates that the button is grayed.
BST_PUSHED establishes that the button is being pressed.
BST_FOCUS defines that the focus is on the button if the value is not NULL.

Support:

→ WinNT 3.1 and higher
→ Win95 and higher
→ WinCE 1.0 and higher

Header file: WINUSER.H

BM_SETCHECK

The BM_SETCHECK message is used to set the selection of a check box or radio button.

```
BM_SETCHECK
wParam = (WPARAM) fCheck;
lParam = 0;
```

➜ I: The value of a constant is expected. This value indicates the desired state of the check box or radio button.
BST_CHECKED specifies that the button is selected.
BST_UNCHECKED specifies that the button is not selected.
BST_INTERMEDIATE establishes that the button is grayed.

➜ O/R: The value NULL is always supplied as the `return value`.

Support:

➜ WinNT 3.1 and higher
➜ Win95 and higher
➜ WinCE 1.0 and higher

Header file: WINUSER.H

BM_SETIMAGE

The BM_SETIMAGE message is sent in order to assign a bitmap or an icon to a button:

```
BM_SETIMAGE
wParam = (WPARAM) fImageType;
lParam = (LPARAM) (HANDLE) hImage;
```

➜ I: `wParam` determines whether a bitmap or an icon is to be assigned.
IMAGE_BITMAP specifies that a bitmap is assigned.
IMAGE_ICOM defines that an icon is assigned.
➜ I: `lParam` is the handle to the bitmap or icon.
➜ A handle to the previously set bitmap or icon is supplied as the `return value`.

Support:

➜ WinNT 4.0 and higher
➜ Win95 and higher
➜ WinCE not supported

Header file: WINUSER.H

BM_SETSTATE

The BM_SETSTATE message determines whether the button should look as if it was clicked or as if it was not clicked:

```
BM_SETSTATE
wParam = (WPARAM) fState;
lParam = 0;
```

→ I: `wParam` determines how the button looks.

TRUE means that the button looks as if it was clicked.

FALSE specifies that the button looks as if it was not clicked.

→ O/R: This message always returns the value NULL.

Support:

→ WinNT 3.1 and higher

→ Win95 and higher

→ WinCE 1.0 and higher

Header file: WINUSER.H

BM_SETSTYLE

The BM_SETSTYLE message changes the properties of a button (these styles replace the old styles, which were specified using the `CreateWindow` function):

```
BM_SETSTYLE
wParam = (WPARAM) LOWORD(dwStyle);
lParam = MAKELPARAM(fRedraw, 0);
```

→ I: `wParam` determines the new properties of the button. These properties can be a combination of all the button properties.

→ I: `lParam` specifies whether the button is to be redrawn.

TRUE defines that the button is to be redrawn.

FALSE specifies that the button should not be redrawn.

→ O/R: This message always supplies the value NULL as the `return value`.

Support:

→ WinNT 3.1 and higher

→ Win95 and higher

→ WinCE 1.0 and higher

Header file: WINUSER.H

Messages from the button to the parent window

WM_COMMAND

The WM_COMMAND message is used to inform the parent window about events. It is used not only by control elements, but also by menus or special keys:

```
WM_COMMAND
wNotifyCode = HIWORD(wParam);
wID = LOWORD(wParam);
hwndCtl = (HWND) lParam;
```

→ O: `wNotifyCode` defines the message more precisely. The *notification* is specified here.

→ O: `wID` determines the ID of the control element. This was specified by `hMenu` in the `CreateWindow` function.

→ O: `hwndCtl` specifies the control element from which the message came.

Support:

→ WinNT 3.1 and higher
→ Win95 and higher
→ WinCE 1.0 and higher

Header file: WINUSER.H

WM_CTLCOLORBTN

The WM_CTLCOLORBTN message is sent so that the parent window can change the color of the button:

```
WM_CTLCOLORBTN
hdcButton = (HDC) wParam;
hwndButton = (HWND) lParam;
```

→ O: `hdcButton` determines the device context of the button.
→ O: `hwndButton` defines the window object of the button.

Support:

→ WinNT 3.1 and higher
→ Win95 and higher
→ WinCE 2.0 and higher

Header file: WINUSER.H

WM_DRAWITEM

The WM_DRAWITEM message is sent if something new is to be drawn for an owner-drawn button:

```
WM_DRAWITEM
idCtl = (UINT) wParam;
lpDrawStruct= (LPDRAWITEMSTRUCT) lParam;
```

→ O: `idCtl` is the ID of the button.
→ O: `lpDrawStruct` is a pointer to a structure of the type DRAW-ITEMSTRUCT.

Support:

→ WinNT 3.1 and higher

→ Win95 and higher
→ WinCE 1.0 and higher

Header file: WINUSER.H

DRAWITEMSTRUCT

The DRAWITEMSTRUCT structure contains information that indicates what has to be redrawn:

```
typedef struct tagDRAWITEMSTRUCT
{
   UINT CtlType;
   UINT CtlID;
   UINT itemID;
   UINT itemAction;
   UINT itemState;
   HWND hwndItem;
   HDC hDC;
   RECT rcItem;
   DWORD itemData;
} DRAWITEMSTRUCT;
```

→ CtlType determines whether a button or another control element is to be redrawn.
ODT_BUTTON specifies that a button is to be redrawn.
ODT_COMBOBOX defines that a combo box is to be redrawn.
ODT_LISTBOX means that a list box is to be redrawn.
ODT_LISTVIEW means that a list view box is to be redrawn.
ODT_MENU specifies that a menu is to be redrawn.
ODT_STATIC means that a text field is to be redrawn.
ODT_TAB determines that a control element is to be redrawn.
→ CtlID defines the ID of the control element to be redrawn.
→ itemID specifies the menu item to be redrawn.
→ itemAction specifies what is to be redrawn.
ODA_DRAWENTIRE declares that everything is to be redrawn.
→ ODA_FOCUS determines whether or not the focus is on the control element.
ODA_SELECT specifies whether the control element was selected or released.
→ itemState determines the state of the control element after it was redrawn.
ODS_CHECKED specifies that the control element was selected.
ODS_COMBOBOXEDIT specifies that a combo box was edited.

ODS_DEFAULT indicates that the control element is the default control element.

ODS_DISABLED specifies that the control element was disabled.

ODS_FOCUS means that the focus is on the control element.

ODS_GRAYED establishes that the control element is grayed.

ODS_SELECTED specifies that the menu item was selected.

→ `hwndItem` defines a handle to the window object.

→ `hDC` defines a handle to a device context.

→ `rcItem` specifies the control element's box.

→ `itemData` contains additional information about the control element.

Support:

→ WinNT 3.1 and higher

→ Win95 and higher

→ WinCE 1.0 and higher

Header file: WINUSER.H

Notification messages

BN_CLICKED indicates that a button was clicked.

BN_DBLCLK/ BN_DOUBLECLICKED specifies that a button was double-clicked.

BN_DISABLE reports that a button was disabled.

BN_HILITE/ BN_PUSHED means that a button was selected.

BN_UNHILITE/ BN_UNPUSHED indicates that a button was released again.

BN_SETFOCUS means that the input focus is on a button.

BN_KILLFOCUS means that a button loses the input focus.

19.1.2   EDIT

An edit field is an input field, which is used to record user entries (see Figure 19.2).

Figure 19.2 *An edit field*

Styles

ES_AUTOHSCROLL automatically jumps ten characters further to the right. You can move to the start of the edit field by pressing Enter.

ES_AUTOVSCROLL scrolls forward one page when you press Enter.

ES_CENTER indicates that the text is centered in `singleline` and `multiline` mode. You can only center text in `singleline` mode in Windows NT 5.0 and Windows 98.

ES_LEFT means that the text is left-aligned.

ES_LOWERCASE specifies that all the characters you enter in the edit field appear in lowercase.

ES_MULTILINE specifies that the edit field can contain a number of lines. An edit field with ES_MULTILINE can contain scroll bars. Normally, edit fields can only contain one line of text.

ES_NOHIDESEL specifies that the entries selected in an edit field remain selected even if the window no longer has the input focus.

ES_OEMCONVERT means that the ANSI text that was entered is converted to the OEM character set and then converted back again.

ES_PASSWORD specifies that all the characters that are entered are replaced by another character (asterisk *).

ES_RIGHT means that the text is right-aligned in a single-line edit field.

ES_UPPERCASE specifies that all the characters you enter in the edit field appear in uppercase.

ES_READONLY means that the user cannot enter any text in the edit field and cannot make any changes.

ES_WANTRETURN specifies that a *carriage return* is inserted in the text. Otherwise, the default push button is activated.

ES_NUMBER means that only numbers can be entered in the edit field.

Messages from the parent window to the edit field

The processing of various standard messages is also specified for the edit fields because this information could be important, e.g. because these messages are also sent to the edit field and can trigger required actions.

EM_CANUNDO

The EM_CANUNDO message is sent in order to get information about whether the last action in the edit field can be undone using the EM_UNDO message:

```
EM_CANUNDO
wParam = 0;
lParam = 0;
```

→ O/R: If EM_UNDO is executed successfully, the value TRUE is returned. Otherwise, the return value is FALSE.

Support:

→ WinNT 3.1 and higher
→ Win95 and higher
→ WinCE 1.0 and higher

Header file: WINUSER.H

EM_UNDO

The EM_UNDO message is sent in order to undo the last action in the edit field:

```
EM_UNDO
wParam = 0;
lParam = 0;
```

→ O/R: The value TRUE is always supplied as the `return value` for a single-line edit field if the function is executed successfully. If the function cannot be executed, the return value is FALSE.

Support:

→ WinNT 3.1 and higher
→ Win95 and higher
→ WinCE 1.0 and higher

Header file: WINUSER.H

EM_CHARFROMPOS

The EM_CHARFROMPOS message is sent in order to get the index of the character and the number of the line:

```
EM_CHARFROMPOS
wParam = 0;
lParam = (LPARAM) (POINTL *) lpPoint;
```

→ I: `lParam` uses a POINT structure to determine the position from which the data is to be returned.
→ O/R: The lower WORD in the value contains the character index. The top WORD contains the line index. All numbering starts at 0.

Support:

→ WinNT 4.0 and higher
→ Win95 and higher
→ WinCE 1.0 and higher

Header file: WINUSER.H

EM_EMPTYUNDOBUFFER

The EM_EMPTYUNDOBUFFER message is sent in order to empty the buffer for the EM_UNDO function:

```
EM_EMPTYUNDOBUFFER
wParam = 0;
lParam = 0;
```

Support:

→ WinNT 4.0 and higher
→ Win95 and higher
→ WinCE 1.0 and higher

Header file: WINUSER.H

EM_FMTLINES

The EM_FMTLINES message is sent so that soft `returns` can be inserted in multi-line edit fields:

```
EM_FMTLINES
wParam = (WPARAM) (BOOL) fAddEOL;
lParam = 0;
```

→ I: `wParam` determines whether soft `returns` may be inserted. The value TRUE indicates that this is permitted, while FALSE means that this is not permitted.

→ O/R: The `return value` corresponds to the value of `wParam`.

Support:

→ WinNT 3.1 and higher
→ Win95 and higher
→ WinCE 1.0 and higher

Header file: WINUSER.H

EM_GETFIRSTVISIBLELINE

The EM_GETFIRSTVISIBLELINE message is sent in order to determine the number of the first line in the edit field:

```
EM_GETFIRSTVISIBLELINE
wParam = 0;
lParam = 0;
```

→ O/R: The index value of the line is supplied as the `return value`. The index value is based on the number 0.

Support:

→ WinNT 3.1 and higher
→ Win95 and higher
→ WinCE 1.0 and higher

Header file: WINUSER.H

EM_GETHANDLE

The EM_GETHANDLE message is sent to an edit field in order to determine the handle of the text buffer of a multi-line edit field:

```
EM_GETHANDLE
wParam = 0;
lParam = 0;
```

→ O/R: The `return value` is a handle to the memory in which the text is stored.

Support:

→ WinNT 3.1 and higher
→ Win95 and higher
→ WinCE 2.0 and higher

Header file: WINUSER.H

EM_GETLIMITTEXT

The EM_GETLIMITTEXT message is sent in order to determine the maximum length of the text:

```
EM_GETLIMITTEXT
wParam = 0;
lParam = 0;
```

→ O/R: The maximum length of the text is supplied as the `return value`.

Support:

→ WinNT 4.0 and higher
→ Win95 and higher
→ WinCE 1.0 and higher

Header file: WINUSER.H

EM_GETLINE

The EM_GETLINE message is sent in order to copy a line of text from an edit field:

```
EM_GETLINE
wParam = (WPARAM) line;
lParam = (LPARAM) (LPCSTR) lpch;
```

→ `wParam` specifies the index of the line. This value is based on NULL. This parameter is ignored for a single-line edit field.
→ `lParam` specifies a pointer to the text buffer.
→ O/R: If the function is executed successfully, it returns the number of characters that were copied.
N: If the number of lines is greater than the number that actually exists, the value NULL is returned.

Support:

→ WinNT 3.1 and higher

→ Win95 and higher

→ WinCE 1.0 and higher

Header file: WINUSER.H

EM_GETLINECOUNT

The EM_GETLINECOUNT message is sent in order to find out the number of lines in a multi-line edit field:

```
EM_GETLINECOUNT
wParam = 0;
lParam = 0;
```

→ O/R: If the function is executed successfully, it returns the number of lines in the edit field. If the edit field does not contain any text, the value 1 is returned.

Support:

→ WinNT 3.1 and higher

→ Win95 and higher

→ WinCE 1.0 and higher

Header file: WINUSER.H

EM_GETMARGIN

The EM_GETMARGIN message is sent in order to determine the width of the left and right margin:

```
EM_GETMARGIN
wParam = 0;
lParam = 0;
```

→ O/R: The bottom word contains the width of the left margin, while the top word contains the width of the right margin.

Support:

→ WinNT 4.0 and higher

→ Win95 and higher

→ WinCE 1.0 and higher

Header file: WINUSER.H

EM_GETMODIFY

The EM_GETMODIFY message is sent in order to find out whether the contents of an edit field was changed:

```
EM_GETMODIFY
wParam = 0;
lParam = 0;
```

➔ O/R: The return value is TRUE if the contents was changed, or FALSE if the contents was not changed.

Support:

➔ WinNT 3.1 and higher
➔ Win95 and higher
➔ WinCE 1.0 and higher

Header file: WINUSER.H

EM_GETPASSWORDCHAR

The EM_GETPASSWORDCHAR message is sent in order to determine the character that is displayed when you enter a password:

```
EM_GETPASSWORDCHAR
wParam = 0;
lParam = 0;
```

➔ O/R: The character is supplied as the return value.
  N: If no character exists, the value NULL is returned.

Support:

➔ WinNT 3.1 and higher
➔ Win95 and higher
➔ WinCE 1.0 and higher

Header file: WINUSER.H

EM_GETRECT

The EM_GETRECT message is sent in order to get information about the size of the box that was set:

```
EM_GETRECT
wParam = 0;

lParam (LPARAM) (LPRECT) lprc;
```
  ➔ I: lParam is the pointer to a RECT structure.

Support:

→ WinNT 3.1 and higher
→ Win95 and higher
→ WinCE 1.0 and higher

Header file: WINUSER.H

EM_GETSEL

The EM_GETSEL message is sent in order to find out the start and end position of the selection:

```
EM_GETSEL
wParam = (WPARAM) (LPDWORD) lpdwStart;
lParam = (LPARAM) (LPDWORD) lpdwEnd;
```

→ O: wParam is a pointer to a WORD value in which the start position is stored.
→ O: lParam is a pointer to a WORD value in which the end position is stored.
→ O/R: The positions are also supplied as the return value. The bottom WORD contains the end position, while the top word contains the start position. The value −1 is returned in special cases.

Support:

→ WinNT 3.1 and higher
→ Win95 and higher
→ WinCE 1.0 and higher

Header file: WINUSER.H

EM_GETTHUMB

The EM_GETTHUMB message is sent so that the position of the scroll box is returned:

```
EM_GETTHUMB
wParam = 0;
lParam = 0;
```

→ O/R: The position of the scroll box is supplied as the return value.

Support:

→ WinNT 3.51 and higher
→ Win95 and higher
→ WinCE 1.0 and higher

Header file: WINUSER.H

EM_GETWORDBREAKPROC

The EM_GETWORDBREAKPROC message is sent in order to get the pointer to the function:

```
EM_GETWORDBREAKPROC
wParam = 0;
lParam = 0;
```

→ O/R: A pointer to a function is returned.
   N: If the function does not exist, the value NULL is returned.

Support:

→ WinNT 3.1 and higher
→ Win95 and higher
→ WinCE not supported

Header file: WINUSER.H

EM_LIMITTEXT

The EM_LIMITTEXT message is sent in order to define the maximum number of characters in an edit field:

```
EM_LIMITTEXT
wParam = (WPARAM) cchMax;
lParam = 0;
```

→ I: wParam specifies the maximum number of characters. If this value is NULL, the value is set to 0x7FFFFFFE for single-line edit fields. The value is set to 0xFFFFFFFF for multi-line edit fields.

Support:

→ WinNT 3.1 and higher
→ Win95 and higher
→ WinCE not supported

Header file: WINUSER.H

EM_LINEFROMCHAR

The EM_LINEFROMCHAR message is sent in order to find the line containing a certain character index in a multi-line edit field:

```
EM_LINEFROMCHAR
wParam = (WPARAM) index;
lParam = 0;
```

→ I: `wParam` specifies the character index. If this value is –1, the position of the caret is returned. If an area is selected, the start position of the selected area is returned instead of the caret.

→ O/R: The index value of the line is returned. This value is based on NULL.

Support:

→ WinNT 3.1 and higher
→ Win95 and higher
→ WinCE not supported

Header file: WINUSER.H

EM_LINEINDEX

The EM_LINEINDEX message is sent in order to determine the character index up to the specified line index:

```
EM_LINEINDEX
wParam = (WPARAM) line;
lParam = 0;
```

→ I: `wParam` is the line index, which is used to return the character index. The value –1 is the current line.

→ O/R: The value of the character index is returned. This value is –1 if the specified line index is greater than the actual line index.

Support:

→ WinNT 3.1 and higher
→ Win95 and higher
→ WinCE 1.0 and higher

Header file: WINUSER.H

EM_LINELENGTH

The EM_LINELENGTH message is sent in order to find out the length of a line. A character index is specified for this:

```
EM_LINELENGTH
wParam = (WPARAM) index;
lParam = 0;
```

→ I: `wParam` specifies the character index.

→ O/R: The length of the line is supplied as the `return value`.

Support:

→ WinNT 3.1 and higher
→ Win95 and higher
→ WinCE 1.0 and higher

Header file: WINUSER.H

EM_LINESCROLL

The EM_LINESCROLL message is sent in order to scroll the text horizontally or vertically:

```
EM_LINESCROLL
wParam = (WPARAM) cxScroll;
lParam = (LPARAM) cyScroll;
```

→ I: wParam specifies the number of characters to be scrolled horizontally.
→ I: lParam specifies the number of characters to be scrolled vertically.
→ O/R: If the message was sent to a multi-line edit field, the value TRUE is returned. If the message was sent to a single-line edit field, the value FALSE is returned.

Support:

→ WinNT 3.1 and higher
→ Win95 and higher
→ WinCE 1.0 and higher

Header file: WINUSER.H

EM_POSFROMCHAR

The EM_POSFROMCHAR message is sent in order to get a description of the co-ordinates by specifying a character index:

```
EM_POSFROMCHAR
wParam = (WPARAM) Index;
lParam = 0;
```

→ wParam is the character index.
→ O/R: The coordinates of the character are returned.

Support:

→ WinNT 4.0 and higher
→ Win95 and higher
→ WinCE 1.0 and higher

Header file: WINUSER.H

EM_REPLACESEL

The EM_REPLACESEL message is sent in order to replace the selected text with the specified text:

```
EM_REPLACESEL
fCanUndo = (BOOL) wParam ;
lpszReplace = (LPCTSTR) lParam ;
```

→ I: wParam specifies whether the function can be undone. TRUE means that the function can be undone, while FALSE means that the function cannot be undone.
→ I: lParam specifies the text to be inserted.

Support:

→ WinNT 3.1 and higher
→ Win95 and higher
→ WinCE 1.0 and higher

Header file: WINUSER.H

EM_SCROLL/ WM_VSCROLL

The EM_SCROLL message is sent in order to scroll the text in a multi-line edit field vertically:

```
EM_SCROLL
wParam = (WPARAM) (INT) nScroll;
lParam = 0;
```

→ nScroll uses a constant to specify how the text is to be scrolled. SB_LINEDOWN means that the text is to be scrolled one line down. SB_LINEUP means that the text is to be scrolled one line up. SB_PAGEDOWN means that the text is to be scrolled one page down. SB_PAGEUP means that the text is to be scrolled one page up.
→ O/R: If the function is executed successfully, the value TRUE is returned in the top WORD. The number of lines actually scrolled is returned in the bottom WORD. FALSE is returned in the event of an error.

Support:

→ WinNT 3.1 and higher
→ Win95 and higher
→ WinCE 1.0 and higher

Header file: WINUSER.H

EM_SCROLLCARET

The EM_SCROLLCARET message is used to get the caret into the edit field:

```
EM_SCROLLCARET
wParam = 0 ;
lParam = 0 ;
```

➜ O/R: A value other than NULL is returned if the message was sent to an edit field.

Support:

➜ WinNT 3.1 and higher
➜ Win95 and higher
➜ WinCE 1.0 and higher

Header file: WINUSER.H

EM_SETHANDLE

The EM_SETHANDLE message is sent in order to set the handle of the memory containing the text for a multi-line edit field:

```
EM_SETHANDLE
wParam = (WPARAM) (HLOCAL) hloc;
lParam = 0;
```

➜ I: wParam is the handle to the memory in which the text is to be stored.

Support:

➜ WinNT 3.1 and higher
➜ Win95 and Win98 are not supported
➜ WinCE 1.0 and higher

Header file: WINUSER.H

EM_SETLIMITTEXT

The EM_SETLIMITTEXT message is sent in order to specify the maximum text length:

```
EM_SETLIMITTEXT
wParam = (WPARAM) Max;
lParam = 0;
```

➜ I: wParam is the maximum length of the text.

Support:

→ WinNT 4.0 and higher
→ Win95 and higher
→ WinCE 1.0 and higher

Header file: WINUSER.H

EM_SETMARGINS

The EM_SETMARGINS message is sent in order to specify the width of the margins of an edit field:

```
EM_SETMARGINS
wParam = (WPARAM) Margin;
lParam = (LPARAM) MAKELONG(wLeft, wRight);
```

→ I: wParam specifies which margin is to be reset. Constants are used to do this.
  EC_LEFTMARGIN means that the size of the left margin is to be reset.
  EC_RIGHTMARGIN means that the size of the right margin is to be reset.
  EC_USEFONTINFO specifies that the size of the margins is set by the font. Single-line edit fields then set the margins to the average character width. Multi-line edit fields set the right margin using the letter A and the left margin using the letter C.
→ lParam specifies the value of the left and right margin.

Support:

→ WinNT 4.0 and higher
→ Win95 and higher
→ WinCE 1.0 and higher

Header file: WINUSER.H

EM_SETMODIFY

The EM_SETMODIFY message is sent in order to indicate whether the edit field was modified:

```
EM_SETMODIFY
wParam = (WPARAM) Modified;
lParam = 0;
```

→ wParam specifies whether the text was modified. If this value is TRUE, the text was modified, but if it is FALSE , the text was not modified.

Support:

→ WinNT 3.1 and higher
→ Win95 and higher
→ WinCE 1.0 and higher

Header file: WINUSER.H

EM_SETPASSWORDCHAR

The EM_SETPASSWORDCHAR message is sent in order to set the password character:

```
EM_SETPASSWORDCHAR
wParam = (WPARAM) (UINT) Character;
lParam = 0;
```

→ I: wParam specifies the character.

Support:

→ WinNT 3.1 and higher
→ Win95 and higher
→ WinCE 1.0 and higher

Header file: WINUSER.H

EM_SETREADONLY

The EM_SETREADONLY message is sent in order to set or not to set ES_READONLY for an edit field:

```
EM_SETREADONLY
wParam = (WPARAM) (BOOL) ReadOnly;
lParam = 0;
```

→ I: ReadOnly determines that ES_READONLY is set or is not set. If this value is TRUE, ES_READONLY is set, but if it is FALSE, ES_READONLY is not set.
→ O/R: This function returns a value other than NULL if it is executed successfully.
    N: The function returns the value NULL if an error occurs.

Support:

→ WinNT 3.1 and higher
→ Win95 and higher
→ WinCE 1.0 and higher

Header file: WINUSER.H

EM_SETRECT

The EM_SETRECT message is sent in order to set the formatted box of an edit field. The edit field is then redrawn:

```
EM_SETRECT
wParam = 0;
lParam = (LPARAM) (LPRECT) lprc;
```

→ I: lParam is a pointer to a RECT structure. The structure defines the size of the box.

Support:

→ WinNT 3.1 and higher
→ Win95 and higher
→ WinCE 1.0 and higher

Header file: WINUSER.H

EM_SETRECTNP

The EM_SETRECTNP message is sent in order to set the formatted box of an edit field. The edit field is not redrawn:

```
EM_SETRECTNP
wParam = 0;
lParam = (LPARAM) (LPRECT) lprc;
```

→ I: lParam is a pointer to a RECT structure, which defines the size of the box.

Support:

→ WinNT 3.1 and higher
→ Win95 and higher
→ WinCE 1.0 and higher

Header file: WINUSER.H

EM_SETSEL

The EM_SETSEL message is sent in order to set the number of selected characters in an edit field:

```
EM_SETSEL
wParam = (WPARAM) (INT) nStart;
lParam = (LPARAM) (INT) nEnd;
```

→ I: wParam specifies the start position.
→ I: lParam specifies the end position.

Support:

→ WinNT 3.1 and higher
→ Win95 and higher
→ WinCE 1.0 and higher

Header file: WINUSER.H

EM_SETTABSTOPS

The EM_SETTABSTOPS message is sent in order to set the tab stops in a multi-line edit field:

```
EM_SETTABSTOPS
wParam = (WPARAM) Tabs;
lParam = (LPARAM) (LPDWORD) lpdwTabs;
```

→ I: wParam determines the number of tab stops.
→ I: lParam determines the tab stops.
→ O/R: If the function is executed successfully, it returns the value TRUE. If an error occurred while executing the function, it returns the value FALSE.

Support:

→ WinNT 3.1 and higher
→ Win95 and higher
→ WinCE 1.0 and higher

Header file: WINUSER.H

Other supported messages

WM_COPY

WM_CUT

WM_PASTE

Messages from the edit field to the parent window

WM_COMMAND

The WM_COMMAND message is used to inform the parent window about events. The WM_COMMAND message is used not only by control elements, but also by menus or special keys:

```
WM_COMMAND
wNotifyCode = HIWORD(wParam);
wID = LOWORD(wParam);
hwndCtl = (HWND) lParam;
```

→ O: `wNotifyCode` defines the message more precisely. The notification message is specified here.
→ O: `wID` determines the ID of the control element. This ID was specified by `hMenu` in the `CreateWindow` function.
→ O: `hwndCtl` specifies the control element from which the message came.

Support:

→ WinNT 3.1 and higher
→ Win95 and higher
→ WinCE 1.0 and higher

Header file: WINUSER.H

WM_CTLCOLOREDIT

The WM_CTLCOLOREDIT message is sent so that the parent window can change the color of the edit field:

```
WM_CTLCOLOREDIT
hdcEdit = (HDC) wParam;
hwndEdit = (HWND) lParam;
```

→ O: `hdcEdit` determines the device context of the edit field.
→ O: `hwndEdit` determines the window object of the edit field.

Support:

→ WinNT 3.1 and higher
→ Win95 and higher
→ WinCE 2.0 and higher

Header file: WINUSER.H

Notification messages

EN_CHANGE specifies that the text in the edit field was changed. The bottom WORD of `wParam` specifies the ID of the edit field. `lParam` determines the handle of the window.

EN_SETFOCUS specifies that the input focus was set for the edit field. The bottom WORD of `wParam` is the ID of the edit field. `lParam` is the handle to the edit field.

EN_UPDATE specifies that the edit field is to be redrawn. This message is sent if the text in the edit field was changed.

EN_HSCROLL indicates that the user clicked the horizontal scroll bar. This message is sent before the edit field is redrawn.

EN_VSCROLL declares that the user clicked the vertical scroll bar. This message is sent before the edit field is redrawn.

EN_MAXTEXT means that the inserted text is too big.

EN_KILLFOCUS means that the edit field no longer has the input focus.

EN_ERRSPACE specifies that there is not enough memory available to execute an action.

19.1.3   List box

A list box is a control element containing a list of items (see Figure 19.3). The user can select any one element in the list. We will now discuss the fundamentals of list boxes in this section.

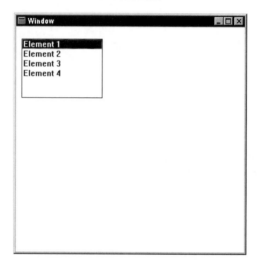

Figure 19.3   *A list box*

Styles

LBS_STANDARD specifies that the elements in the list box are sorted alphabetically. The parent window receives input if you click or double-click an element.

Messages from the parent window to the list box

LB_GETCURSEL

The LB_GETCURSEL message is sent in order to get the index of the currently selected element:

```
LB_GETCURSEL
wParam = 0;
lParam = 0;
```

→ O/R: The index of the selected element is returned. This index is based on the value 0. If no entry is selected, the value LB_ERR is returned.

Support:

→ WinNT 3.1 and higher
→ Win95 and higher
→ WinCE 1.0 and higher

Header file: WINUSER.H

LB_GETCOUNT

The LB_GETCOUNT message is sent in order to find out the number of elements in a list box:

```
LB_GETCOUNT
wParam = 0;
lParam = 0;
```

→ O/R: If the function is executed successfully, it returns the number of elements in the list box. If an error occurs, the value LB_ERR is returned.

Support:

→ WinNT 3.1 and higher
→ Win95 and higher
→ WinCE 1.0 and higher

Header file: WINUSER.H

LB_ADDSTRING

The LB_ADDSTRING message is sent in order to add a string to a list box. If LBS_SORT is not set, the string is added at the end of the list:

```
LB_ADDSTRING
wParam = 0;
lParam = (LPARAM) (LPCTSTR) lpsz;
```

→ I: lParam is the text of the new element.
→ O/R: The value of the index of the string is returned. If an error occurs, the value LB_ERR is returned. If there is not enough space to store the string, the value LB_ERRSPACE is returned.

Support:

→ WinNT 3.1 and higher
→ Win95 and higher
→ WinCE 1.0 and higher

Header file: WINUSER.H

LB_DELETESTRING

The LB_DELETESTRING message is sent in order to delete a string in a list box:

```
LB_DELETESTRING
wParam = (WPARAM) index;
lParam = 0;
```

→ I: wParam specifies the index of the string to be deleted.
→ O/R: The number of strings remaining in the list is returned. If an error occurs, the value LB_ERR is returned.

Support:

→ WinNT 3.1 and higher
→ Win95 and higher
→ WinCE 1.0 and higher

Header file: WINUSER.H

Messages from the list box to the parent window

WM_COMMAND

The WM_COMMAND message is used to inform the parent window about events. It is used not only by control elements, but also by menus or special keys:

```
WM_COMMAND
wNotifyCode = HIWORD(wParam);
wID = LOWORD(wParam);
hwndCtl = (HWND) lParam;
```

→ O: wNotifyCode defines the message more precisely. The notification message is specified here.
→ O: wID determines the ID of the control element. This ID was specified by hMenu in the CreateWindow function.
→ O: hwndCtl specifies the control element from which the message came.

Support:

→ WinNT 3.1 and higher
→ Win95 and higher
→ WinCE 1.0 and higher

Header file: WINUSER.H

WM_CTLCOLORLISTBOX

The WM_CTLCOLORLISTBOX message is sent so that the parent window can change the color of the list box:

```
WM_CTLCOLORLISTBOX
hdcListBox = (HDC) wParam;
hwndListBox = (HWND) lParam;
```

→ O: hdcListBox specifies the device context of the list box.
→ O: hwndListBox specifies the window object of the list box.

Support:

→ WinNT 3.1 and higher
→ Win95 and higher
→ WinCE 2.0 and higher

Header file: WINUSER.H

Notification messages

LBN_DBLCLICK specifies that an element in the list box was double-clicked. This message is only sent using LBS_NOTFIY.

19.1.4   Static

General information

A *Static* control element is a text field. A text field displays text (see Figure 19.4). Unlike the simple TextOut function, this text is retained when you move the window.

Figure 19.4 *A text field*

Styles

SS_SIMPLE specifies that a simple box containing left-aligned text is displayed.

Messages from the parent window to the text field

There are no important messages.

Messages from the text field to the parent window

WM_COMMAND

The WM_COMMAND message is used to inform the parent window about events. It is used not only by control elements, but also by menus or special keys:

```
WM_COMMAND
wNotifyCode = HIWORD(wParam);
wID = LOWORD(wParam);
hwndCtl = (HWND) lParam;
```

→ O: wNotifyCode defines the message more precisely. The notification message is specified here.
→ O: wID determines the ID of the control element. This ID was specified by hMenu in the CreateWindow function.
→ O: hwndCtl specifies the control element from which the message came.

Support:

→ WinNT 3.1 and higher
→ Win95 and higher
→ WinCE 1.0 and higher

Header file: WINUSER.H

WM_CTLCOLORSTATIC

The WM_CTLCOLORSTATIC message is sent so that the parent window can change the color of the text field:

```
WM_CTLCOLORSTATIC
hdcStatic = (HDC) wParam;
hwndStatic = (HWND) lParam;
```

→ O: hdcStatic specifies the device context of the text field.
→ O: hwndStatic specifies the window object of the text field.

Support:

→ WinNT 3.1 and higher
→ Win95 and higher
→ WinCE 2.0 and higher

Header file: WINUSER.H

Notification messages

STN_CLICKED specifies that the text field was clicked once.

STN_DBLCLK specifies that the text field was double-clicked.

Part III

Go ahead!

DirectX

20.1 General information

DirectX is a new API that provides graphics and sound functions. These graphics functions are very fast because they allow better access to the hardware. DirectX allows device-independent programming and improved hardware selection. And this improved hardware access makes it easier to develop games with graphics and sound, which are very demanding when it comes to system performance.

The DirectX API is created using C++ objects (see also Chapter 22). It is therefore important to differentiate between Windows and C++ objects.

In this chapter, we will look at a more complex sample program, which describes the basic properties of DirectX.

20.2 A DirectX program

20.2.1 General information

This program is intended to show clearly how fast graphics are created without errors. This procedure is applied in practically all modern games. We will create a memory for storing all the graphics, which will be drawn exclusively in this memory. We will then write the entire memory into the screen memory. If all the graphics are transferred in an identical way, we will have delays. The last graphic always has the shortest dwell time in the screen memory. See Figure 20.1.

Primary Buffer

Figure 20.1 *The application after you start it*

20.2.2   The source code

```
#include <windows.h>
#include <ddraw.h>

LPDIRECTDRAW7 lpDD=NULL;
LPDIRECTDRAWSURFACE7 lpDDSPrimary=NULL;
LPDIRECTDRAWSURFACE7 lpDDSBack=NULL;

int Array = 1;

LRESULT CALLBACK WindowProc(HWND, unsigned,
                                  WPARAM, LPARAM);


int APIENTRY WinMain(HINSTANCE hInstance,
                  HINSTANCE hPrevInstance,
                  LPSTR     lpCmdLine,
                  int       nCmdShow)
{
    WNDCLASS wc;
    wc.style = CS_HREDRAW | CS_VREDRAW;
    wc.lpfnWndProc = (WNDPROC) WindowProc;
```

```
wc.cbClsExtra = 0;
wc.cbWndExtra = sizeof(DWORD);
wc.hInstance = hInstance;
wc.hIcon = NULL;
wc.hCursor = LoadCursor(NULL, IDC_ARROW);
wc.hbrBackground = (HBRUSH)
                    GetStockObject(BLACK_BRUSH);
wc.lpszMenuName = NULL;
wc.lpszClassName = "WinProg";

RegisterClass(&wc);

int ScreenWidth = GetSystemMetrics(SM_CXSCREEN);
int ScreenHeight = GetSystemMetrics(SM_CYSCREEN);

HWND hWnd;

hWnd = CreateWindow("WinProg",
                    "DirectX Program",
                    WS_POPUP,
                    0,
                    0,
                    ScreenWidth,
                    ScreenHeight,
                    NULL,
                    NULL,
                    hInstance,
                    NULL);

ShowWindow(hWnd, nCmdShow);

UpdateWindow(hWnd);


ShowCursor (false);

SetTimer (hWnd, NULL, 1000, NULL);

DirectDrawCreateEx(NULL, (void **) &lpDD,
                   IID_IDirectDraw7, NULL);
lpDD->SetCooperativeLevel(hWnd, DDSCL_EXCLUSIVE |
                          DDSCL_FULLSCREEN );
```

```
lpDD->SetDisplayMode( 640, 480, 16, 0, 0);

DDSURFACEDESC2 ddsd;
ZeroMemory(&ddsd,sizeof(ddsd));
ddsd.dwSize = sizeof( ddsd );
ddsd.dwFlags = DDSD_CAPS | DDSD_BACKBUFFERCOUNT;
ddsd.ddsCaps.dwCaps = DDSCAPS_PRIMARYSURFACE |
                      DDSCAPS_FLIP |
                      DDSCAPS_COMPLEX;
ddsd.dwBackBufferCount = 1;

lpDD->CreateSurface( &ddsd, &lpDDSPrimary, NULL );

DDSCAPS2 ddscaps;
ZeroMemory(&ddscaps,sizeof(ddscaps));
ddscaps.dwCaps=DDSCAPS_BACKBUFFER;

lpDDSPrimary->GetAttachedSurface(&ddscaps,&lpDDSBack);


    MSG msg;

    while (GetMessage(&msg, NULL, 0, 0))
    {
        TranslateMessage( &msg );
        DispatchMessage( &msg );
    }

lpDDSBack->Release ();
lpDDSPrimary->Release ();

lpDD->Release ();

ShowCursor (true);

return msg.wParam;

}

LRESULT CALLBACK WindowProc(HWND hWnd,
                            unsigned uMsg,
                            WPARAM wParam,
```

```
                       LPARAM lParam)
{
    switch (uMsg)
    {
        case WM_TIMER:
            if (Array == 1)
            {
                HDC hdc;
                lpDDSBack->GetDC (&hdc);
                TextOut (hdc, 10, 10,
                         "Primary Buffer        ",
                         lstrlen("Primary Buffer        "));
                lpDDSBack->ReleaseDC (hdc);
                Array = 2;
            }
            else
            {
                HDC hdc;
                lpDDSBack->GetDC (&hdc);
                TextOut (hdc, 10, 10, "Back Buffer        ",
                         lstrlen("Back Buffer        "));
                lpDDSBack->ReleaseDC (hdc);
                Array = 1;
            }
            lpDDSPrimary->Flip(0,DDFLIP_WAIT);
            return 0;
        case WM_KEYDOWN:

            DestroyWindow (hWnd);
            return 0;
        case WM_DESTROY:
            PostQuitMessage(0);
            break;
         default:
             return DefWindowProc(hWnd, uMsg,
                                  wParam, lParam);
    }
    return 0;
}
```

20.2.3 Explanation of the source code

Initialization

```
DirectDrawCreateEx(NULL, (void **) &lpDD,
                   IID_IDirectDraw7, NULL);
lpDD->SetCooperativeLevel(hWnd, DDSCL_EXCLUSIVE |
                          DDSCL_FULLSCREEN );
lpDD->SetDisplayMode( 640, 480, 16, 0, 0);

DDSURFACEDESC2 ddsd;
ZeroMemory(&ddsd,sizeof(ddsd));
ddsd.dwSize = sizeof( ddsd );
ddsd.dwFlags = DDSD_CAPS | DDSD_BACKBUFFERCOUNT;
ddsd.ddsCaps.dwCaps = DDSCAPS_PRIMARYSURFACE |
                      DDSCAPS_FLIP |
                      DDSCAPS_COMPLEX;
ddsd.dwBackBufferCount = 1;

lpDD->CreateSurface( &ddsd, &lpDDSPrimary, NULL );

DDSCAPS2 ddscaps;
ZeroMemory(&ddscaps,sizeof(ddscaps));
ddscaps.dwCaps=DDSCAPS_BACKBUFFER;

lpDDSPrimary->GetAttachedSurface(&ddscaps,&lpDDSBack);
```

A DirectDraw object is created first.

This object is then linked to the window and Full Screen mode is enabled.

The graphics card settings are defined (resolution, color, etc.).

The first Surface object is created. This is the screen memory. This is then linked to the DirectDraw object as well.

The second Surface object is created next. This is a simple memory object in which the program will draw. It is linked to the first Surface object.

The main part

```
if (Array == 1)
        {
            HDC hdc;
            lpDDSBack->GetDC (&hdc);
            TextOut (hdc, 10, 10,
                    "Primary Buffer         ",
```

```
                      lstrlen("Primary Buffer          "));
        lpDDSBack->ReleaseDC (hdc);
        Array = 2;
   }
   else
   {
        HDC hdc;
        lpDDSBack->GetDC (&hdc);
        TextOut (hdc, 10, 10, "Back Buffer          ",
                 lstrlen("Back Buffer          "));
        lpDDSBack->ReleaseDC (hdc);
        Array = 1;
   }
   lpDDSPrimary->Flip(0,DDFLIP_WAIT);
```

The program draws in the second surface memory. Either "Primary Buffer" or "Back Buffer" is written in. The old GDI function can still be used. DirectX objects can also return a device context.

The second surface memory overwrites the entire first surface memory. Bitmaps from the previous chapters were used.

Deinitialization

```
lpDDSBack->Release ();
    lpDDSPrimary->Release ();
    lpDD->Release ();
```

All the objects are now released from the memory. The most dependent object must be released first. The objects must be released in this sequence.

20.3 DirectX and bitmaps

20.3.1   General information

This program demonstrates how to use bitmaps with DirectX. See Figure 20.2.

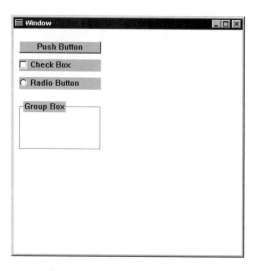

Figure 20.2 *The application after you start it*

20.3.2 The source code

```
#include <windows.h>
#include <ddraw.h>


LPDIRECTDRAW7 lpDD=NULL;
LPDIRECTDRAWSURFACE7 lpDDSPrimary=NULL;
LPDIRECTDRAWSURFACE7 lpDDSBack=NULL;
LPDIRECTDRAWSURFACE7 lpBitmap=NULL;
LPDIRECTDRAWSURFACE7 lpBitmapp=NULL;

int Array = 1;

LRESULT CALLBACK WindowProc(HWND, unsigned,
                            WPARAM, LPARAM);
LPDIRECTDRAWSURFACE7 bitmap_surface(LPCTSTR);


int APIENTRY WinMain(HINSTANCE hInstance,
                     HINSTANCE hPrevInstance,
                     LPSTR     lpCmdLine,
                     int       nCmdShow)
{
    WNDCLASS wc;
```

```
wc.style = CS_HREDRAW | CS_VREDRAW;
wc.lpfnWndProc = (WNDPROC) WindowProc;
wc.cbClsExtra = 0;
wc.cbWndExtra = sizeof(DWORD);
wc.hInstance = hInstance;
wc.hIcon = NULL;
wc.hCursor = LoadCursor(NULL, IDC_ARROW);
wc.hbrBackground = (HBRUSH)
                    GetStockObject(BLACK_BRUSH);
wc.lpszMenuName = NULL;
wc.lpszClassName = "WinProg";
RegisterClass(&wc);

int ScreenWidth = GetSystemMetrics(SM_CXSCREEN);
int ScreenHeight = GetSystemMetrics(SM_CYSCREEN);

HWND hWnd;


hWnd = CreateWindow("WinProg",
                    "DirectX Program",
                    WS_VISIBLE | WS_POPUP,
                    0,
                    0,
                    ScreenWidth,
                    ScreenHeight,
                    NULL,
                    NULL,
                    hInstance,
                    NULL);

ShowWindow(hWnd, nCmdShow);

UpdateWindow(hWnd);

ShowCursor (false);

SetTimer (hWnd, NULL, 1000, NULL);

DirectDrawCreateEx(NULL, (void **) &lpDD,
                    IID_IDirectDraw7, NULL);
```

```
lpDD->SetCooperativeLevel(hWnd, DDSCL_EXCLUSIVE |
                          DDSCL_FULLSCREEN );
lpDD->SetDisplayMode( 640, 480, 16, 0, 0);

DDSURFACEDESC2 ddsd;
ZeroMemory(&ddsd,sizeof(ddsd));
ddsd.dwSize = sizeof( ddsd );
ddsd.dwFlags = DDSD_CAPS | DDSD_BACKBUFFERCOUNT;
ddsd.ddsCaps.dwCaps = DDSCAPS_PRIMARYSURFACE |
                      DDSCAPS_FLIP |
                      DDSCAPS_COMPLEX;
ddsd.dwBackBufferCount = 1;

lpDD->CreateSurface( &ddsd, &lpDDSPrimary, NULL );


DDSCAPS2 ddscaps;
ZeroMemory(&ddscaps,sizeof(ddscaps));
ddscaps.dwCaps=DDSCAPS_BACKBUFFER;

lpDDSPrimary->GetAttachedSurface(&ddscaps,&lpDDSBack);


lpBitmap = bitmap_surface ("bitmap.bmp");
lpBitmapp = bitmap_surface ("bitmapp.bmp");



    MSG msg;

    while (GetMessage(&msg, NULL, 0, 0))
    {
        TranslateMessage( &msg );
        DispatchMessage( &msg );
    }

lpBitmapp->Release ();
lpBitmap->Release ();
lpDDSBack->Release ();
lpDDSPrimary->Release ();
```

```
        lpDD->Release ();

        ShowCursor (true);

        return msg.wParam;


}




LRESULT CALLBACK WindowProc(HWND hWnd, unsigned uMsg,
                            WPARAM wParam, LPARAM lParam)
{
    switch (uMsg)
    {
      case WM_TIMER:
         RECT rects;
         rects.top = 0;
         rects.left = 0;
         rects.right = 639;
         rects.bottom = 479;
         if (Array == 1)
         {
            lpDDSBack->BltFast (0,0,lpBitmap,&rects,
                              DDBLTFAST_NOCOLORKEY);
            Array = 2;
         }
         else
         {
            lpDDSBack->BltFast (0,0,lpBitmapp,&rects,
                              DDBLTFAST_NOCOLORKEY);
            Array = 1;
         }
         lpDDSPrimary->Flip(0,DDFLIP_WAIT);
         return 0;
      case WM_KEYDOWN:
         DestroyWindow (hWnd);
         return 0;
```

```
            case WM_DESTROY:
               PostQuitMessage(0);
               break;
            default:
                return DefWindowProc(hWnd, uMsg,
                                        wParam, lParam);
      }
      return 0;

}


LPDIRECTDRAWSURFACE7 bitmap_surface(LPCTSTR file_name)
{
   HDC hdc;
   HBITMAP bit;
   LPDIRECTDRAWSURFACE7 surf;

   bit=(HBITMAP)
   LoadImage(NULL,
            file_name,
            IMAGE_BITMAP,
            0,0,
            LR_DEFAULTSIZE | LR_LOADFROMFILE);

   if (!bit) return NULL;
   BITMAP bitmap;
   GetObject( bit, sizeof(BITMAP), &bitmap );
   int surf_width=bitmap.bmWidth;
   int surf_height=bitmap.bmHeight;


   HRESULT ddrval;
   DDSURFACEDESC2 ddsd;
   ZeroMemory(&ddsd,sizeof(ddsd));
   ddsd.dwSize = sizeof(DDSURFACEDESC2);
   ddsd.dwFlags = DDSD_CAPS | DDSD_WIDTH | DDSD_HEIGHT;
   ddsd.ddsCaps.dwCaps =
   DDSCAPS_OFFSCREENPLAIN|DDSCAPS_SYSTEMMEMORY;
   ddsd.dwWidth = surf_width;
```

```
        ddsd.dwHeight = surf_height;

        ddrval=lpDD->CreateSurface(&ddsd,&surf,NULL);



        if (ddrval!=DD_OK)
        {
            DeleteObject(bit);
            return NULL;

        }
        else
        {
            surf->GetDC(&hdc);

            HDC bit_dc=CreateCompatibleDC(hdc);

            SelectObject(bit_dc,bit);

            BitBlt(hdc,0,0,
                    surf_width,surf_height,
                    bit_dc,0,0,SRCCOPY);

            surf->ReleaseDC(hdc);
            DeleteDC(bit_dc);
        }

        DeleteObject(bit);

    return surf;
    }
```

UNICODE 21

21.1 General information

UNICODE is the successor of ANSI. UNICODE is a 16-bit character set that supports 65,536 different characters in one character set. All the characters of the world are represented in the first 30,000 or so characters. The Win32 API contains functions that support both UNICODE and ANSI code. For example, the `CreateWindow` function is available as the `CreateWindowA` and `CreateWindowW` functions. A function is selected in the background by a default setting.

21.2 Operating systems

21.2.1 Windows 95

The system uses ANSI. We recommend that you use ANSI.

21.2.2 Windows 98

The system uses ANSI. It is possible to use UNICODE, but we recommend that you use ANSI.

21.2.3 Windows NT

You can use ANSI, but this slows the system down because the system uses UNICODE. All text must be converted beforehand. We recommend that you use UNICODE.

21.2.4 Windows 2000

You can use ANSI, but this slows the system down because the system uses UNI-CODE. All text must be converted beforehand. We recommend that you use UNI-CODE.

21.2.5 Windows CE

You must use UNICODE because the system only uses UNICODE.

COM 22

22.1 General information

This chapter is not intended as a guide to programming, but briefly describes what COM is and what it is used for.

COM is an object standard and means *Component Object Model* (model for the development of object components). COM is also called a binary standard. It is a standard for objects. This standard can be used by practically all languages (C++, Pascal, Basic and so on). Data in a COM object is changed using the methods in the COM object. The collection of methods is called the Interface. There is a standard API. This API contains functions that you can use to create a COM object and to get a pointer to COM objects, which is used in the same way as a real C++ object. A COM object is created by an ID, which specifies what is to be created for a COM object.

22.2 DirectX

DirectX also uses COM objects. This is why you first search by ID in order to get a pointer to an object. All DirectX versions are overwritten and even the old programs run with the new DirectX files to which new objects are simply added. DirectDraw is an example of this. There are a number of different Direct-Draw objects:

1 IDirectDraw
2 IDirectDraw2
3 IDirectDraw4
4 IDirectDraw7

DirectX can be used by C++, Pascal, and Visual Basic thanks to COM.

Before COM was introduced, users could only write functions that could be used by other languages. Now, COM has even made it possible to write objects that can also be used by other languages.

Resources

23.1 General information

Resources are data entries stored in the EXE or DLL file.
This data is not part of the application, but is additional data that is supplied to the application.

This data is described by a text file ("*resource definition file*"). This file contains references to the individual icons, bitmaps, etc. A resource compiler can be used to combine this data to form a single binary file. This is appended to the EXE or DLL file.

Resources are used in two ways. On the one hand, the application itself can use them and make objects from them. All the resources have a value that identifies them uniquely. You can determine this value from the resource.h file. On the other hand, however, resources are also used by other applications. Displaying files is a good example of this – in this case, a file is displayed using a symbol or icon. This icon is stored as a resource in the file.

Some DLL files, e.g. font files, consist only of resources.

23.2 An example of a resource

23.2.1 General information

This program creates a window. This window is linked to an icon resource and a cursor resource.

Source code of the main file

```
#include <windows.h>
#include "resource.h"


LRESULT CALLBACK WndProc (HWND, UINT, WPARAM, LPARAM);
```

```
int APIENTRY WinMain(HINSTANCE hInstance,
                     HINSTANCE hPrevInstance,
                     LPSTR     lpCmdLine,
                     int       nCmdShow )
{
   WNDCLASS WndClass;
   WndClass.style = 0;
   WndClass.cbClsExtra = 0;
   WndClass.cbWndExtra = 0;
   WndClass.lpfnWndProc = WndProc;
   WndClass.hInstance = hInstance;
   WndClass.hbrBackground = (HBRUSH) (COLOR_WINDOW+1);
   WndClass.hCursor = LoadCursor (hInstance,
                         MAKEINTRESOURCE(IDC_CURSOR1));
   WndClass.hIcon = LoadIcon (hInstance,
                       MAKEINTRESOURCE(IDI_ICON1));
   WndClass.lpszMenuName = 0;
   WndClass.lpszClassName = "WinProg";

   RegisterClass(&WndClass);

   HWND hWindow;
   hWindow = CreateWindow("WinProg","Window",
                     WS_OVERLAPPEDWINDOW,
                     0,0,600,400,NULL,NULL,
                     hInstance, NULL);

   ShowWindow (hWindow, nCmdShow);

   UpdateWindow (hWindow);

   MSG Message;
   while (GetMessage(&Message, NULL, 0, 0))
   {

      TranslateMessage (&Message);
      DispatchMessage(&Message);
   }

   return (Message.wParam);
}
```

```
LRESULT CALLBACK WndProc (HWND hWnd, UINT uiMessage,
                         WPARAM wParam,LPARAM lParam)
{
   switch(uiMessage)
   {
      case WM_DESTROY:
         PostQuitMessage(0);
         return 0;
      default:
         return DefWindowProc (hWnd, uiMessage,
                               wParam, lParam);
   }
}
```

Source code of the resource file

```
#define IDI_ICON1                      101
#define IDC_CURSOR1                    102

#ifdef APSTUDIO_INVOKED
#ifndef APSTUDIO_READONLY_SYMBOLS

#define _APS_NEXT_RESOURCE_VALUE       129
#define _APS_NEXT_COMMAND_VALUE        32771
#define _APS_NEXT_CONTROL_VALUE        1000
#define _APS_NEXT_SYMED_VALUE          110
#endif
#endif
```

Source code of the script file

```
#include "resource.h"

LANGUAGE LANG_ENGLISH, SUBLANG_ENGLISH

#pragma code_page(1252)

IDI_ICON1 ICON DISCARDABLE "icon1.ico"

IDC_CURSOR1 CURSOR DISCARDABLE "cursor1.cur"
```

23.2.2   Explanation

MAKEINTRESOURCE

The MAKEINTRESOURCE macro turns an integer value into a value that specifies the resource.

Loading resources

To load a resource using the `LoadIcon` and `LoadCursor` functions, you must specify the instance handle.

A

ANSI 31, 42
ANSI_FIXED_FONT 56
ANSI_VAR_FONT 55
applications 119
ASCII code 31

B

BeginPaint 23, 176
BitBlt 83
bitmap fonts 31
BITMAPFILEHEADER 89
BITMAPINFO 89
Bitmaps 75
block graphics 31
BM_GETCHECK 225
BM_GETIMAGE 225
BM_GETSTATE 226
BM_SETCHECK 226
BM_SETIMAGE 227
BM_SETSTATE 227
BM_SETSTYLE 228
BMP file 85
BN_CLICKED 41
Borland C++ 5.5 3
Brush object 22, 26, 28, 190, 202
BS_CHECKBOX 73
BS_GROUPBOX 73
BS_RADIOBUTTON 73
BUTTON 41, 73, 222–231

C

check boxes 73, 223
CloseHandle 118, 215
color depth 76
COLORREF 22
COM 275
CombineRgn 195
compilers 3
Component Object Model 275

control element 41
    creating 46
    edit field 53
    WM_COMMAND 48
CopyFile 217
CreateBitmap 82
CreateCompatibleDC 82
CreateFile 116, 212
CreateMenu 103
CreatePen 22, 187
CreateRectRgn 194
CreateSolidBrush 22, 189
CreateStruct 158
CreateThread 123
CreateWindow 10, 41, 154
creating the window 10
cursor 21

D

DDB 75
DEFAULT_GUI_FONT 55
DefWindowProc 15, 16
DeleteDC 84
DeleteFile 218
DeleteObject 189
Description 202
DestroyWindow 159
determining directories 106
device context object 17, 176
Device-Dependent Bitmap 75
device-dependent bitmap 75
Device-Independent Bitmap 75
device-independent bitmap 75
DIB 75, 85
DirectX 259
DispatchMessage 13, 168
displaying graphics 17
displaying text 31, 205
DLL files 125, 277
DllMain 129

DOCINFO 145
DRAWITEMSTRUCT 230
DrawText 37, 198
Dynamic Link Library 125

E

EDIT 53, 61, 232–249
edit field 53
ellipse 28, 186
EM_CANUNDO 233
EM_CHARFROMPOS 234
EM_EMPTYUNDOBUFFER 234
EM_FMTLINES 235
EM_GETFIRSTVISIBLELINE 235
EM_GETHANDLE 235
EM_GETLIMITTEXT 236
EM_GETLINE 236
EM_GETLINECOUNT 237
EM_GETMARGIN 237
EM_GETMODIFY 237
EM_GETPASSWORDCHAR 238
EM_GETRECT 238
EM_GETSEL 239
EM_GETTHUMB 239
EM_GETWORDBREAKPROC 240
EM_LIMITTEXT 240
EM_LINEFROMCHAR 240
EM_LINEINDEX 241
EM_LINELENGTH 241
EM_LINESCROLL 242
EM_POSFROMCHAR 242
EM_REPLACESEL 243
EM_SCROLL 243
EM_SCROLLCARET 244
EM_SETHANDLE 244
EM_SETLIMITTEXT 244
EM_SETMARGINS 245
EM_SETMODIFY 245
EM_SETPASSWORDCHAR 246
EM_SETREADONLY 246
EM_SETRECT 247
EM_SETRECTNP 247
EM_SETSEL 247
EM_SETTABSTOPS 248
EndDoc 146
EndPage 146
EndPaint 23, 29, 177
EXE file 119, 277
ExitWindowsEx 73

F

file 109
    create new 115
    open 115
file systems 109
FillRect 28, 185
Font object 35

G

GDI 17
GDI fonts 31
GetClientRect 82
GetCurrentDirectory 107
GetDeviceCaps 106, 178
GetMessage 13, 161
GetPixel 181
GetStockObject 35, 197
GetTextMetrics 49
GetWindowDC 180
GetWindowsDirectory 107
Graphics Device Interface 17
group boxes 73, 223

H

HANDLE 9
HFONT 35
HMENU 103
HWND 10

I

icon 21
InsertMenuItem 103
ISO 8859 31
ISO standard 31

L

LB_ADDSTRING 251
LB_DELETESTRING 252
LB_GETCOUNT 251
LB_GETCURSEL 250
LineTo 26, 183
List box 250
LoadCursor 21
LoadIcon 21
loading resources 280
lstrcat 37
lstrcmp 37, 63
lstrcpy 37
lstrlen 37

M

memory device context object 76
menu 93
    creating 101
MENUITEMINFO 104
message loop 12
message processing 15
message structure 14
MoveFile 218
MoveToEx 25, 181
MS Visual C++ 6.0 4
MSG 14
multitasking 12
multi-threading 119

N

non-proportional font 31
NTFS 109

O

object 10, 16
OEM character set 31
OEM_FIXED_FONT 56
Or 11

P

PAINTSTRUCT 24, 178
PeekMessage 162
Pen object 23, 26, 28, 188, 202
POINT 182
PolyBezier 184
PolyLine 183
PostQuitMessage 15
predefined fonts 35
predefined window classes 221
PRINTDLG 143
PrintDlg 143
printers 139
process 119
proportional font 31
Protected Fat File System 109
prototype of the function 15
push button 223

R

radio buttons 73, 223
ReadFile 117, 215
RECT 24, 186
Rectangle 26, 185
Region object 195

regions 208
RegisterClass 10, 164
ReleaseDC 179
resource definition file 277
resources 277
return value from the application 15
RGB colors 76
RGB macro 22, 194
RoundRect 27

S

scan codes 31, 42
screen device context object 76
SelectObject 25, 36, 188
SetBkColor 36, 37, 191
SetBkMode 193
SetDIBitsToDevice 90
SetMenu 105
SetPixel 180
SetRect 27
SetTextAlign 37, 192
SetTextColor 36, 37, 191
SetTimer 134, 137
SetWindowRgn 196
ShowWindow 12, 160
source code 170, 200, 208
standard Print dialog box 143
StartDoc 145
StartPage 146
Static 253
StretchBlt 84
string functions 37
switch 15
switch branching 15
system shutdown 65
SYSTEM_FONT 42, 54

T

TerminateThread 124
TEXTMETRIC 50
TextOut 36, 38, 190
thread 119
timer function 135
timer messages 131
timers 131
TranslateMessage 167
True Color 76
TrueType fonts 31

U

UNICODE 273
UpdateWindow 12
Using Regions 208

V

vector fonts 31

W

Win32 API 17
   data types 149
   file management 211
   GDI 173
   Windows fundamentals 153
Window class 8
Window object 154
Windows.h 7
WinMain 8
WM_COMMAND 41, 48, 106, 228, 248,
   252, 254
WM_CREATE 46, 157
WM_CTLCOLORBTN 229
WM_CTLCOLOREDIT 249
WM_CTLCOLORLISTBOX 253
WM_CTLCOLORSTATIC 255
WM_DESTROY 15, 159
WM_DRAWITEM 229
WM_GETTEXT 61
WM_LBUTTONDOWN 81
WM_PAINT 22, 41, 168, 200
WM_QUIT 15
WM_RBUTTONDOWN 84
WM_TIMER 134
WM_VSCROLL 243
WNDCLASS 8, 164
WndProc 15
WriteFile 117, 216
WS_CHILD 61